Help Your Child Learn to Read

Help Your Child Learn to Read

New Ways to Make Learning Fun

DR. HARRY W. FORGAN

Pagurian Press Limited

Cover and photographs on pages 6, 10, 22, 37, 44, 78, 94, 107, 120, by
Miller Services Limited. Photo on page 128 by Steckley Photography.

Distributed by
Publishers Marketing Group
A Baker & Taylor Company
Executive Offices
1515 Broadway, New York, N.Y. 10036

Distribution Center
Gladiola Avenue, Momence, Ill. 60954

ISBN 0-88932-000-4 cloth
0-88932-018-7 paper

Printed and bound in the United States of America.

*To our moms and dads
for helping Ruth Ann and me learn to read,
and with hope that we in turn
can help Jimmy and Jennifer enjoy the values of reading*

CONTENTS

PREFACE

This book is for parents of preschool and elementary school children who are concerned about their child's reading achievement. Research indicates that home background is one of the most important factors determining success in reading achievement. Dedicated teachers cannot provide for all the individual differences of students — their achievement range is simply too great. Parents can and must (a) help their child value reading, (b) show interest in their child's reading achievement, and (c) provide the basic necessities and practice activities which make it possible for children to learn to read. This book describes how parents can assume these three major responsibilities.

The ideas in this book are designed to help parents take advantage of teachable moments which occur daily. A cure-all method for learning to read is not presented — there is no such thing. Rather, basic guidelines, practical ideas, games, and activities are given, which, if implemented according to the suggested guidelines for working with your child, will increase his reading achievement and love for reading.

Gone are the days when schools discouraged parents from helping their children. Now teachers realize that the cooperation of parents is essential for a child to succeed in reading. The mysteries of reading instruction have been eliminated as schools seek the cooperation of parents both at home and at school as school volunteers. This book then is also designed for use by school volunteers who can use the ideas and guidelines with the children they are assigned to help. Teachers too will find this book a valuable resource for suggesting ideas and explaining the nature of the reading skills to parents and school volunteers. Parents and school volunteers can be *partners* with teachers and thus increase the likelihood of more children learning to read successfully.

A variety of ideas, games, and activities are presented, so that parents and school volunteers can get involved to the degree they wish, based upon the child's needs and how much time is available for helping. The parents will find that the emphasis is not on turning the home into a miniature school, but rather on having fun with their child as his reading achievement improves. School volunteers will also be satisfied with the

11

reactions of the children they are teaching because the children will think they are "playing games" rather than doing what sometimes can be labeled "laborious school work."

Chapter One is devoted to how you can use this book effectively to get the most out of it. All users of the book — parents, school volunteers, and teachers — are urged to read Chapter One first. A glance at the contents of Chapters Two through Nine will reveal the specific reading skills children develop during the preschool and elementary school years. Each of these chapters is replete with guidelines, ideas, games, and activities to aid you in helping your child accomplish the most important reading skills. Chapter Ten presents the causes of reading failure and where to seek aid for children who need specialized help.

I want to acknowledge the teachers, parents, and students who have shared ideas and suggestions for this book. A special word of appreciation is extended to those parents who evaluated the manuscript and provided many valuable reactions: my sister, Carol Ann Hartong, and friends, Mary Scalf, John and Gail Nelson, Mary Ann Stefko, Zody Fogarty, Betty Heenan, and Chuck Mangrum.

Janice Gross and Philip Kellerman, two of my students at the University of Miami, deserve special thanks for their help in preparing Appendices B and G. The editors of Pagurian Press Limited offered valuable editorial remarks which I appreciated.

Most important, I want to thank my wife, Ruth Ann, for her valuable assistance. When I first considered writing a book for parents I proposed that we co-author the book since she is a former elementary school teacher and a marvelous mother. We discussed the possibility and finally decided I should author the book. As I look at the final draft, I see her influence throughout every chapter. Ruth Ann shared many ideas, and offered constructive suggestions in addition to drawing the illustrations and typing the many rough copies and final manuscript. The support and encouragement she offered as she worked by my side made the book possible.

Our children, Jimmy and Jennifer, are to be thanked for their cooperation as we worked with them without letting them know this book was designed for parents to help their children learn to read. I hope you have as much fun using the ideas, games, and activities with your children.

CHAPTER ONE

PARENTS CAN HELP—HERE'S HOW

So you want to help your child learn to read! Your concern for your child's success in reading is important. Reading is the foundation of nearly every school subject. It opens the doors to a richer and more independent life by making available exciting adventures, valuable information, and interesting ideas. The child who learns to read well is indeed fortunate. You want to make sure *your* child develops this important skill.

Why Parents Can and Must Help

As a classroom teacher I encouraged parents to help their children in reading. Parents are important in helping since so many natural opportunities arise when learning can occur. Children are constantly asking, "What does this say?" or "How do you spell ———?" When going places and doing things with your child there are many opportunities for learning. Even questions that arise when watching television programs can provide a valuable vehicle for increasing reading skills. Many "teachable moments" are lost if parents do not know what skills are involved in reading and how to nourish them.

A second reason why parents should help their children is that teachers have an impossible job when attempting to provide for all the individual differences within the typical classroom. Even at the first-grade level, children vary greatly in reading achievement. This range in achievement continues to increase and by the time children are in sixth grade the teacher can expect them to differ at least nine years in reading achievement. It is simply impossible for a teacher to provide for the individual differences of some thirty children. Parents, on the other hand, can work with their child on a one-to-one basis. This is not to say that parents must be responsible for teaching their children to read, but rather that cooperation from parents is necessary for the child to reach his full potential. The schools cannot and never will be able to do the entire job.

What Parents Can Do

Generally, parents have three major responsibilities in helping their child learn to read. *One basic responsibility is that of helping the child value books and reading.* Research has shown that parents who read to their child and provide many books and magazines, or make use of the public library, help their child to develop an interest in and love for reading. The child who enjoys listening to stories and is surrounded by good books and magazines learns to enjoy reading and realizes the value of it. Of course a favorable attitude toward books is essential for achievement in reading.

A second responsibility that parents have is to show interest in their child's reading. Reading in our society is considered to be a task all children should achieve. As with other basic behaviors, children want adults and other significant people to notice their achievements. Parents who look at their child's school papers and go to the school occasionally to talk with the teacher, show their child they are interested. Another way parents can show their interest is by helping their child practice the new skills in reading which he is developing. Finally, parents show interest by seeking specialized help if it is necessary for their child.

The final responsibility is to provide for the physical, social, emotional, and language needs of their children. Physical factors such as good vision, hearing, and health are essential for effective growth in reading. Parents are expected to help their child maintain his health by getting the proper rest and diet. Many times parents are the first ones to become aware of vision or hearing problems and have the responsibility of seeking further diagnosis. Social-emotional growth of children is very important to the reading process, too. Parents are expected to love and accept their child as he is. In addition to accepting and loving the child, the parent should help the child develop appropriate relationships so other family members, friends, and peers will accept and love him. Parents are expected to provide a variety of experiences in which language skills develop naturally. The parents who do many things with their child and talk about the experiences they are having are actually helping their child learn to read.

If you will look back at the three basic responsibilities of parents you will notice the initial letters in the key words form the abbreviation VIP. In other words, one responsibility is for parents to help their children *value* books and reading. Second, parents should show *interest* in their child's reading. Finally, parents should *provide* the basic necessities that are needed for achievement in reading. I believe the abbreviation VIP describes the role of parents in helping their child learn to read; parents are VIP's. Thousands of research studies have revealed parents are one of the most important factors in determining whether or not children learn to read. You are a VIP.

14

How This Book Can Help You Be a VIP

As parents of a preschool and an elementary school child, and former elementary school teachers, my wife and I have noticed the many natural opportunities which arise daily in which we can help our children. This book was written to share some of the techniques we are using with our children and have recommended to parents of our students. The book consists of specific examples of how parents can fulfill the VIP role.

One of the parents who field-tested many of the ideas said, "I think the activities are all useful and worthwhile and there is enough variety that parents can get involved just to the degree they feel they can, depending upon individual circumstances." I was happy to hear this reaction because the book is organized so that it can be used in different ways depending upon: (1) the amount of time parents have available to help their child, and (2) the amount of help the child needs. Some parents have more time and/or a child who needs more help. Other parents may not have as much time and/or a child who needs a considerable amount of assistance. The format and organization of the book were planned so it can be used by all parents — "depending upon individual circumstances."

As you examine the chapters, you will realize they are organized according to the major objectives of reading instruction. A bird's eye view of the contents and purpose of each chapter follows.

Chapter One is devoted to how the book is organized and general guidelines for working with your child effectively. Before going on to other chapters, become thoroughly acquainted with the arrangement of ideas in this book so you can use those which are most valuable to your child at this time. Also, the general guidelines for helping your child which are presented near the end of the chapter are important so you can actually enjoy helping him. *Warning: Read Chapter One carefully before using the ideas in this book*.

The second chapter is especially for parents of preschool, kindergarten, and first grade children. Parents and educators realize that the first years of life are perhaps the most important. There are so many things that parents can do to help their children develop the readiness skills which enable children to learn words. The readiness skills are explained in Chapter Two along with many ideas for helping your child develop these in natural situations in the home.

Chapter Three is devoted to techniques to help your child use phonics to sound out words. Phonics has always been an important concern of parents. Most parents believe instruction in phonics is essential to help children recognize words. Since approximately 85 percent of the words in the English language follow the principles of phonics, this is a very important part of reading. General guidelines, as well as specific ideas, are presented so you can help your child apply phonics.

In addition to using phonics to recognize words, children learn in four other ways how to recognize words. Chapter Four presents ideas on how you can help your child develop a large sight vocabulary consisting of words that appear frequently and words which cannot be sounded out using phonics. This chapter also has ideas on how you can help your child look at the structure of the word and use context clues as other ways of figuring out the pronunciation and meanings of words. Finally, Chapter Four provides many suggestions on how you can help your child use a dictionary to find the pronunciation and meanings of new words.

Being able to pronounce or recognize words is useless unless the child comprehends. Chapter Five shows how you can help your child in this respect. Reading is the process of getting meaning from printed symbols, not simply calling words.

Vocabulary is perhaps one of the most important factors that influences reading achievement. Sixty percent of comprehension is accounted for by vocabulary. Parents have long realized the importance of vocabulary and are aware of their influence in helping their child extend his vocabulary. Chapter Six has many words that you may want your child to learn, as well as suggestions for helping your child extend his vocabulary in natural situations. Again the emphasis is on parents taking advantage of teachable moments which occur daily.

Most parents enjoy listening to their child read orally but are concerned about whether or not the child is developing silent reading skills and appropriate rates of reading. Chapter Seven will help you understand the characteristics of an effective oral and silent reader as well as guidelines for helping your child develop these skills. Suggestions as to how you can help your child develop flexible rates of reading are also presented.

As children progress through the elementary school years, "reading to learn" becomes more important than learning to read. In other words, upper-grade children use reading as a source of gathering information. Chapter Eight is designed to enable you to help your child develop appropriate study skills at an early age. There is also emphasis in this chapter on helping your child use textbooks and reference books to their best advantage. Research has shown that elementary school children can develop many study skills and skills in using reference materials early in their school years.

There are some children who avoid reading. If you are an avid reader, you realize the value of being able to read. Even if you have not read a book during the past year, you do read every day as you move about your home and community. There are recipes to be read and important signs along the roads and highways. You want your child to be interested in reading so he can live a richer and more independent life. Chapter Nine is devoted to helping your child develop and extend his interests in reading.

A special note concerning Chapter Ten is needed since it does not have the same format as the other chapters. Chapter Ten deals with the factors which determine whether or not your child learns to read or how well he learns to read. If your child is having difficulty, consult this chapter for sources of help which are available.

There are many appendices, most of which contain further ideas and/or sources of games, activities, or books valuable in helping your child become an effective reader. In addition, there are some tests to see what your child knows about phonics and other aids which will help you get the most out of this book.

The Arrangement of Ideas, Games, and Activities in This Book

Now that you are aware of what this book contains, it is time to notice the arrangement of the ideas. You will notice Chapters Two through Nine include a description of the skills in the introductory section of the chapters. All parents are advised to read these descriptions so they will have a better understanding of the many skills that are involved in reading. The introduction to each chapter then provides the background information concerning the skills which will enable you to help your child.

Many games, ideas, and activities you can use to help your child develop particular skills follow the concise description of the skills. You will notice these games, ideas, and activities are numbered consecutively throughout Chapters Two to Nine. The numbering of the activities makes it possible for you to refer to particular activities easily.

As you look at the games, ideas, and activities, you will notice that some of them are starred with an asterisk. These are the most important ideas in the book — *ones that all parents should use.* A comprehensive list indicating the starred ideas (which enable you to be a VIP) are presented in Appendix J for easy reference. If your time is limited, or if your child does not need as much help because he is progressing well in reading, use the starred activities to insure that your child continues to progress.

The numbered games, ideas, and activities which are not starred are also valuable. These are presented especially for parents who have more time to work with their child *or* have a child who needs more assistance.

As you skim through the chapters in this book, you will notice that the numbered ideas, games, and activities also include a letter or letters. You will see the letters a, b, c, ab, bc, or abc. *These letters indicate the level at which the skills are usually emphasized.* The following definitions are used to indicate when the skills are generally appropriate:

a — preschool, kindergarten, first grade
b — second and third grade
c — fourth, fifth, and sixth grade
ab — preschool through third grade, depending upon the complexity of materials, ideas, words, and so forth
bc — second grade through sixth grade, depending upon the complexity of materials, ideas, words, and so forth
abc — all age levels from preschool to sixth grade, depending upon the complexity of the materials, ideas, words, and so forth

For your convenience, you will find a graded list of the activities for each of the three major grade level areas (a b and c) in Appendix J.

You can use Appendix J to determine which activities are most appropriate for your child. If your child is a preschooler, kindergartner, or first grader, or if your child is on the readiness or first-grade level, regardless of the actual grade placement, use the a, ab, and abc activities. If your child is on the second or third grade reading level use the b, bc, and abc activities. Finally, if your child is on the fourth, fifth, or sixth grade reading level, select the appropriate c, bc, and abc activities.

A Word of Caution

As was mentioned earlier, *children differ greatly in reading achievement.* Your child might be in the first grade and be able to read at the fourth grade level; or in the fourth grade and is reading at the first grade level. Use the a, b, c, codes as clues to grade placement of the ideas, games, and activities, but you must consider *your child* as the final and most important factor when selecting activities. Be sure to show your child's teacher this book and assure her of the fact that you have read the guidelines for working with your child.

Ask the teacher to tell you the two most important things you need to help him: (a) most important skill needs in reading, and (b) his reading level. A form you can use as you confer with your child's teacher follows. In addition to completing the form, the teacher may want to check certain activities she believes would be valuable for your child.

Most teachers are delighted that you are willing to help. Gone are the days when teachers thought you might do more harm than good. The parents who serve as school volunteers have demonstrated the fact that *parents* can help children achieve at higher levels in reading and other content areas. Furthermore, research indicates parents have been able to help their own children at home. There is no doubt about it, parents are VIP's in helping children learn to read.

Guide to Parent-Teacher Conferences Concerning Reading

Directions to parents: Take this book to the prearranged conference with your child's teacher. Show it to her and explain that you would like to help your child practice the reading skills he is learning. Ask her to indicate his reading level and then check *no more than three areas* in which your child needs the most assistance at this time. Assure your child's teacher that you have read the suggested guidelines for helping your child.

Directions to teacher: Indicate the child's reading level and check no more than three areas in which the child needs the most practice and reinforcement at this time. You may want to add comments to indicate particular problems the child is encountering. For example, if you check consonant sounds you may want to specify certain sounds.

Child's Name .... Date ....

Child's reading level .... Kindergarten/first grade (a)

(check one) .... Second/third grade (b)

.... Fourth/fifth/sixth grade (c)

Reading Skills (check no more than three) *Comments/Suggestions*

Readiness (Chapter Two)

.... 1. Listening and Speaking Vocabularies

.... 2. Concept Development

.... 3. Visual Skills

.... 4. Auditory Skills

.... 5. Interest in Words and Books

.... 6. Names of Letters

Phonics (Chapter Three)

.... 1. Consonant Sounds and Generalizations

.... 2. Sound Patterns

.... 3. Vowel Sounds and Generalizations

.... 4. Syllabication and Accent

Other Word Recognition Techniques (Chapter Four)

.... 1. Sight Words

.... 2. The Structure of Words

.... 3. Context Clues

.... 4. Dictionary Skills

Comprehension Skills (Chapter Five)

.... 1. Main Idea

.... 2. Significant Details

.... 3. Sequence of Events

.... 4. Drawing Conclusions

.... 5. Evaluating Critically

Vocabulary Development (Chapter Six)

.... Level a (Kindergarten/first grade)

.... Level b (second/third grade)

.... Level c (fourth, fifth, or sixth grade)

Oral and Silent Reading Skills (Chapter Seven)

.... 1. Oral Reading Skills

.... 2. Silent Reading Skills

.... 3. Rate of Reading

Locational and Study Skills (Chapter Eight)

.... 1. Study Skills and Habits

.... 2. Reference Skills

.... 3. Skills for Reading Content Materials

Interest in Reading (Chapter Nine)

.... 1. Expand Interest in ....

.... 2. Develop Interest in ....

Do you believe my child needs specialized help? What kind? Why? (Chapter Ten)

What other suggestions do you have for me as I assist my child?

How to Know what Ideas, Games, and Activities to Use

In addition to the preceding general guidelines for selecting ideas, games, and activities you can use, the following specific suggestions will enable you to select the most important ones for *your* child.

Parents of a Preschool Child

1. Read the remainder of this chapter and the introductions to Chapters Two through Ten. Concentrate on Chapter Two.
2. If your child is enrolled in a preschool program, arrange a conference using the Parent/Teacher Conference Guide. Normally the teacher will indicate level "a" and then specify the readiness skills which the child needs to develop. If so, use the "a" activities in Chapter Two concerning the particular skills the teacher recommends. For example, she may say visual skills, listening vocabulary, and concept development. If so, use the "a" activities for these skill areas. If your preschooler is beginning to read words, the teacher will probably suggest using the a, ab, and abc activities in the first section of Chapter Four concerning sight words, then Chapter Three concerning phonics, then back to the other appropriate (a, ab, abc) parts of Chapter Four, and Chapters Five, Six, Seven, Eight, and Nine. A summary list of the a, ab, and abc activities which are found in the different chapters is found in Appendix J.
3. If your child is not enrolled in a preschool program, do the "a" activities in Chapter Two first. If your child seems ready to read words follow the sequence which was suggested in Number 2 above.
4. Read Chapter Ten if your child seems to be experiencing problems with vision, hearing, language.
5. Remember, if your time is limited, or if you have a child who does not need as much guidance, do only starred a, ab, and abc activities for which your child seems ready.

Parents of an Elementary School Child

1. Read the remainder of this chapter and the introductions to Chapters Two through Ten.
2. Arrange a conference with your child's teacher to determine (a) his reading level and (b) specific skill needs in reading. Use the Guide to Parent/Teacher Conferences in Reading.
3. On the basis of your conference, select appropriate activities to use with your child. For example, if the teacher says your child is on

20

second grade level and needs help with vowel sounds, main idea, and oral reading skills, refer to the appropriate sections of this book using Appendix J and then use the activities in each skill area labelled b, bc, abc (b indicates second and third grade level).

4. Do the starred activities if your time is limited and/or if your child needs only limited help in reading. If you have more time and/or a child who needs more help, do many of the appropriate activities concerning the skills the teacher suggests.

5. Other ways of determining your child's needs and levels are to (a) look at his report card to see if it indicates his reading level and major skill needs, or (b) look at the papers your child is bringing home to see what skills are being emphasized (the skill is usually listed at the bottom or side of the page), and (c) use the phonics tests in Appendix A and then select activities to help your child overcome any weaknesses.

6. Refer to Chapter Ten if your child is not making progress in learning to read.

School Volunteers Working with Preschool or Elementary School Children

1. Use the Guide to Parent/Teacher Conferences to determine the (a) reading levels and (b) most important reading skills the child or children assigned to you need to develop.

2. Select (and adapt if necessary) the ideas which are appropriate according to the child's level (a, b, or c) and skill needs. For example, if the teacher says the child is reading at the beginning of the first grade level and needs help with auditory skills, names of the letters, and sight words, look at Appendix J for these skill areas and then select the a, ab, or abc activities which seem most appropriate and suit the child's interests.

3. Read Chapter Ten to understand why some children have difficulty in reading and some sources of help which are available.

General Guidelines for Helping Your Child

A few years ago my wife and I decided we could save money by buying a home barber kit. After purchasing the kit, my wife glanced at the booklet of instructions and said she was ready to cut my hair. I replied, "Wait a minute! You did not even read the instructions!" She assured me there was "nothing to it" and so I could do nothing but sit back and pray. Of course, the results were disastrous!

The above situation is analogous to helping your child. You must read and think about the following guidelines for helping your child or your results will be disastrous. Remember the warning: *Read Chapter One carefully before using the ideas in this book.* I believe the guidelines which follow are the most important pages.

21

School volunteers must become aware of the young child's short attention span.

There are some basic techniques all parents should follow. If you implement these guidelines your child will be happy and you will realize just how satisfying teaching can be. If you neglect these techniques your child will be unhappy and you will realize how frustrating teaching can be! Periodically review these suggestions so the help that you give your child will be valuable and rewarding.

a. *Praise your child sincerely and avoid using sarcasm.* Your child wants to please you and show you that he is learning. Phrases such as "great," "you're on your toes," and "I like that because ———" are extremely important if related in a sincere way. Nonverbal ways of praising such as a pat on the back, kiss, or a wink, are just as important as words. Never use sarcasm or belittlement. Phrases such as "you'll never learn," "you just can't read," "you're not like your sister," lead the child to develop the concept that he is a failure and cannot learn. Realize how much power you have as a parent in helping your child develop his self-concept. The phrase, "If a child lives with approval, he learns to like himself," is trite, but so true. Always be positive in your approach.

b. *Use games, ideas, and activities in informal ways as opportunities naturally arise in the home.* Remember it is not necessary to set a specific time and a place to work on reading. Your child does not have to be sitting at a desk or a table while you force him to work. Select those activities that you know your child will enjoy. Some activities in this book may be exciting to some children and boring to others. Also, notice many of the ideas are designed for helping your child as you are riding in the car, waiting for something, watching television, or playing on the floor. Do not turn your home into a miniature school. You can have many enjoyable as well as productive hours with your child if you keep this important guideline in mind.

c. *Watch the attention span of your child.* It is so important to know the meaning of "enough." Plan to stop an activity before the child is tired of it so he will want to play it again. If you use a variety of activities and ideas with your child, chances are you will enjoy the time you spend together. When you explain words to your child, notice his reactions so you do not tell more than necessary. Periodically reread the possible ideas which are appropriate for your child's needs and select the ones which you believe are in line with his interests and attention span.

d. *Be patient when working with your child.* Reading is a very difficult task. For example, try to read the following sentence which uses symbols that are different from the regular alphabet.

⊥ΔΤ⍴⊸ℇΠ   ΔΤ⍴   ⌞∪⌞ᑌΤℇΔ⌀ℇ.

You will find this impossible to read unless I tell you that p is represented by ⊥, a by Δ , r by Τ, e by ⍴ , n by ⊸, t by ℇ , s by Π, i by ⌀, m by ∪, and o by ⌞ᑌ . If you had to learn an entirely new alphabet, you would realize how much practice and repetition are necessary. The average child requires several repetitions to learn a word so he can respond to it automatically when he sees it. Of course, many repetitions are also needed for a child to learn particular sounds, names of letters, and study skills. Do not expect your child to learn everything the first, second, or third time you try. You must be tolerant and patient.

e. *Make sure your child is successful.* All children as well as adults like to be successful. For example, I continue to play one song on the organ because I can play that song well. When I try new songs, I make many errors and immediately switch back to the song I can play perfectly. I realize that I am not going to be an accomplished organist. Unfortunately, a child does not have the option of saying he does not want to be an accomplished reader. Our society demands that its citizens be able to read. This being the case, try to use activities, ideas, and words with which the child can be successful. This is not to say the child will get every item right, but he should be getting 90 percent of the items correct, otherwise he will become easily frustrated and begin to feel a failure. You will readily determine what things your child can do successfully and then you can make alterations upon your observations.

f. *Accept your child as he is and do not pressure him too much.* If your child is in the fourth grade and is still working on many of the skills which are taught in the first grade, it is not because he wants to be behind. He does not like to hear you tell others about any problems that he might be experiencing in reading. Every child has strengths and weaknesses. If your child is progressing well in reading, this guideline probably does not mean too much to you. Conversely, if your child is experiencing problems in learning to read, this is one of the most important guidelines.

g. *Make learning meaningful.* Try to help your child realize how he can use the information or skill he is learning. For example, children should know they are learning to divide words into syllables because it is necessary to do so before a word can be sounded out. If a child does not realize the reasons for what he is learning, he will not be able to apply the skills. Continue to ask your child or point out why he is learning a particular skill or knowledge. This does not mean that you should spend lots of time trying to lecture to your child about the importance of some skill. Again the "let's play a game" approach which is used in this book is stressed rather than "it's now time to work on reading." Research has shown that children do learn via games and enjoy them. The simple question, "How is this going to help you?" can be used to implement this guideline effectively.

h. *Do not be overly concerned about your child's reading achievement.* The parent who buys every reading device and material hinders the child. The parent-child relationship is very beautiful. You should take advantage of all the aspects of it by making sure that you do many things with your child. If you overemphasize reading the child will rebel. If you are not having fun together as you use the ideas in this book, evaluate yourself by rereading the above guidelines. You must avoid doing more harm than good.

i. *Fathers should help too!* The term "parents" refers to a mother and father. Unfortunately, not all children have both parents, but if your child does, dad should help, too. This is especially true if your child is a boy. Elementary school age males generally view reading as a feminine activity, and these are the most important years of sex role identification. Perhaps this in part accounts for the fact that 9 out of 10 remedial readers are males. Fathers who do accept the VIP responsibilities can attest to the fact that reading stories to their son or daughter and doing things together are very enjoyable and satisfying experiences.

This book, then, provides the necessary information for you to assume the three responsibilities you have in helping your child become an excellent and avid reader. You will find many ideas for helping your child *value* reading, practical suggestions for showing *interest* in your child's reading achievement, and guidelines for *providing* for the physical, social-emotional, and language needs of your child. You can be a VIP in helping your child learn to read. Have fun and faith in yourself as you fulfill your VIP role.

24

CHAPTER TWO

HELPING YOUR CHILD DEVELOP THE READINESS SKILLS

Understanding the Readiness Skills

There are some skills your child must develop before he learns words. These are often called readiness skills because they help the child get ready for reading. Readiness skills are usually developed in nursery school, kindergarten, and in some first grades. At the same time, you should remember there are some older children who may need more work on the readiness skills. If your child is in the second or third grade and is experiencing difficulty in learning to read, the teacher may suggest using some of the ideas in this chapter. Suggestions are presented for helping your child develop his speaking and listening vocabulary, concepts, visual skills, auditory skills, interest in words and books, and the names of letters.

Your child needs to learn to listen and say many words before he learns to read words. Of course the more words the child is able to listen to and understand or say, the better he will be able to read. For example, if your child sees the written word "banana," and has never heard any-one use this word, it will not mean anything to him. Your child's *speaking and listening vocabularies* must be expanded before a reading vocabulary is developed.

Concept development is related closely to speaking and listening vocabularies. Your child must learn concepts or associate mental images with words before he can get meaning from words. Dad realizes the importance of background information when he tries to read a cookbook which includes many terms which he may not understand. When Mother attempts to read a car-care manual she understands the needs of knowing the different parts of an automobile. Children also encounter this dilemma when they try to read stories about something they cannot visualize. If your child is reading a story about picking apples and does not have a mental image of an apple or an apple tree, he will not understand what he reads. It is important then that your child develop as many concepts or mental images as possible. Only then will he be able to read words with understanding.

Reading is a *visual process* since printed symbols are involved. Visual motor coordination is required so both eyes work together as they move from left to right to follow a printed line of words. In addition to focusing on words, children must be able to see differences in words and letters. Reading words in the English language requires some fine visual discrimination, such as telling the differences among the letters b, p, q, and d. Visual discrimination is a difficult skill for children to develop so we usually begin with large discriminations such as in geometric shapes. As the child progresses, he learns to discriminate different words, such as "bad" and "dad." Of course children must be able to mentally picture the letters so they can begin to associate them with particular names and sounds. Visual memory is also essential to help your child remember words.

Before your child can begin to associate particular sounds with symbols, he must be able to hear differences among the sounds and remember sounds. This may seem like a pretty simple task to us as adults, but it is difficult for children to notice the difference between sounds which are similar, such as those which are represented by the symbols b and d. In addition to hearing differences in sounds, children must be able to remember sounds and associate them with particular symbols. Auditory memory makes it possible for children to say a certain sound when they see a letter. These *auditory skills* are necessary before instruction in phonics takes place. A child cannot sound out a word if he cannot distinguish and remember the sounds of the letters that make up the word.

Another pre-reading skill is developing *interest in words and books*. Before you can teach words to your child, he must have some desire for knowing what the words say. If your child is not asking, "What does that say?" he is not going to learn words as quickly as children who are motivated. In addition to displaying interest in words, your child must develop interest in books and learn some of the fundamental information concerning books. He soon learns that books have a top and bottom, front and back, and that words and sentences go from left to right. As simple as this may seem to adults, the importance of these skills is readily noticed if you have ever observed a one-year-old child who is looking at a book upside down.

The final pre-reading skill is learning the *names of letters*. Knowledge of the names of each letter is useful in learning to read because teachers usually refer to the letters by their names rather than by their sounds. Even though there are 26 letters in our alphabet, children must learn more than 26 letters because capital and small letters are sometimes different. For example, the lower case a and the capital A are extremely different. As you are helping your child learn the names of letters, be sure to print the letters rather than writing (cursive) them or you will be introducing even more symbols. A guide for letter formation is presented near the end of this chapter.

As you read the descriptions of the readiness skills, you have probably noticed these skills are expanded throughout the school years. A child continues to improve his speaking and listening vocabularies, develops new concepts, and acquires more skill in making fine visual and auditory discriminations. Although most of these activities are designated with a "lower case a" indicating they are most appropriate for preschool, kindergarten and first grade children, many of these skills are expanded during the child's elementary school years. Your task right now is only to help your child develop the readiness skills which will enable him to read some words. Your child will let you know "when the time is ripe" by asking you to write words or by trying to read and spell words. It will be at this time that you will be ready for Chapters Three and Four of this book.

Once when famed educator Francis Wayland Parker finished one of his lectures a mother asked, "How early can I begin the education of my child?" Parker asked, "When will the child be born?" "Born?" the mother replied, "she is five years old." Parker responded by saying, "My goodness woman, don't stand here talking to me, hurry home, you have lost the best five years."

Today we realize more than ever before the importance of the first few years of life. Studies show children can and do remember more than we ever thought possible. You are his first and his most important teacher! Remember the guidelines which were suggested in Chapter One and have fun as you use the practical suggestions that follow.

Listening and Speaking Vocabularies

*1a. *Dinner Time.* Often natural opportunities arise during the dinner hour to help your child learn new words. As different members of the family describe their activities, words are used which are new to the preschool child. When your child asks what a particular word means, give a brief explanation and then try to use the word later on in the evening or on the following day. Remember that a child needs many meaningful repetitions with the word to make it his own.

2a. *Mother Says.* This little game is similar to "Simon Says." Your child should follow your directions only when they are preceded by the phrase, "Mother says." For example, you might say, "Mother says sit down." Praise your child when he follows your directions if they are preceded by "Mother says." You can work on other readiness skills such as left to right orientation by saying, "Mother says raise your right hand." This activity may be valuable when your child is picking up the toys in his room. Often children will respond to directions when they are presented in game form.

3ab. *What Am I?* Describe some object your child knows. Have him listen carefully and guess what you are describing, with as few clues as possible. For example, you might say, "I am round, red, and have seeds inside. I'm used to make cider. What am I?" By introducing some new

---

*Remember the asterisks which appear in front of the numbered ideas, games, and activities indicate the most important ones. Read Chapter One for definitions of a, b, and c.

knowledge along with familiar facts, your child's world expands. This activity is especially useful when waiting for someone or riding in a car.

*4a. *Listening to Stories.* Reading stories to your child is a very valuable activity. This helps him develop listening comprehension in addition to expanding concepts and providing hours of enjoyment. Stop as you read and ask questions about the pictures, characters, or events in the story. You might also have your child dramatize part of the story or retell his favorite part. Take your child to the store or library with you when you select books. Use books with many pictures so the child is developing concepts as you read.

*5ab. *Listening to Records.* Records are useful when you are too busy to read to your child. They also introduce him to other voices and sounds. Some records are accompanied by picture books for the child to follow. Other records are available which ask children to listen to and follow directions. Suggest a purpose for listening. A list of some records you may want to use can be found in Appendix C.

*6a. *Talking with Your Child.* Most adults enjoy using baby talk with infants, but as your child develops, avoid using baby talk. Your child will experience difficulty in sounding out words if he cannot say them correctly. Remember not to talk down to your child because children learn new words by hearing them. As you use unfamiliar words, define them in simple terms. Your child will let you know when he does not understand or has had enough of a description.

7a. *Puppets, Pets, and Play Telephones.* Children will often talk to pets when they will not talk to adults. This is also true of puppets, play telephones, and dolls. Provide these toys to encourage your child to talk. Words and sentence structure are learned after many meaningful repetitions.

*8abc. *Go Places with Your Child.* Experiences stimulate speaking and provide opportunities to expand listening vocabulary. Take your child with you when you go shopping, bicycle riding, or simply walking around the block. Children enjoy talking about flowers, trees, birds, stars, and other people. New and exciting experiences such as the circus, miniature golf, ball games, trips to the waterfront, and so forth are valuable. Life is exciting, and as an adult you can relive it as you notice many of the things you have taken for granted. As you see new things, talk informally with your child about them. Vocabulary is best developed through direct experiences.

*9abc. *Read Stories and Poems which Have New Words.* As you are reading stories you may want to substitute familiar words for some of the words your child does not understand. But you should also provide simple explanations of new words so your child's vocabulary increases. Pictures often can help you explain new words. In providing explanations, adults usually tell children more than they want to know. Watch the reactions of your child so you will know when you have said enough.

10a. *Using Pictures.* Ask your child to explain or tell a story about pictures he has drawn, photographs, or pictures in magazines. Avoid asking questions that are too specific and require only a one-word answer.

Open-ended questions such as, "What is happening here?" or "Tell me about this," may elicit more oral communication. Specific questions can be asked to help your child notice details.

*11abc. *Sentence Structure.* Ask your child to talk about experiences he has had when you were not with him. Repeat words or sentences he uses incorrectly by saying them correctly when he is finished. He will become frustrated and avoid talking if you correct him while he is talking or trying to explain or describe something. Make sure you are patient as your child is trying to find the correct words, and supply words that the child may not be able to think of. Of course your facial expressions will in part provide the praise he deserves.

12a. *Have Your Child "Read" Stories to You.* Many children like to "read" stories based on their memory while using the pictures for guides. Providing opportunities for this encourages speaking skills. You will also get an idea of your child's listening comprehension and imagination. Take time to listen to your child.

13ab. *Round Robin.* Begin a story by saying one sentence such as, "Once there was a little girl." Your child and other family members can then add a sentence as it becomes their turn. Continue until you have a complete story. This activity is especially fun when riding in a car.

14ab. *Tape Recordings.* Cassette tape recorders are relatively inexpensive when compared to the price of some of the toys which are available for children. Purchase or borrow a recorder and have your child make a tape to send to a relative or friend. Both listening and speaking skills will be developed if you play the tape for the child.

*15ab. *Can You Tell Me Another Story?* Children enjoy the times when you cuddle them and tell them a story. You can help increase your child's listening vocabulary if you use new words and describe the new words as a natural part of the story. For example, if you are telling a story about a child who lost his pet and you use the word "shaggy," make sure you provide a simple definition of shaggy in the next sentence or two. As you describe why the dog was called shaggy, your child will be learning the definition of a new word.

*16ab. *We Had a Nice Day.* As you are tucking your child into bed, review the events of the day. Children enjoy this time together and it provides an opportunity to reinforce new words the child has learned during the day. Remember your child's listening and speaking vocabularies are developed by having many experiences with a new word.

*17abc. *Using Synonyms.* You can help your child expand his vocabulary by using a new word and then later on in the sentence, or in the following sentence, use a familiar word which means the same as the new word. Let us suppose you are eating breakfast with your child and he says, "My eggs are still hot." You might respond by saying, "Yes, eggs do retain their heat for a long time," and follow this by the sentence, "They stay hot for a while." In doing so, you will be helping your child realize that retain and stay are synonyms. You can do this frequently throughout the day as you take advantage of teachable moments.

29

Concept Development

*18abc. *Experiences Make the Difference!* Children develop concepts by experiencing many situations. The child who has visited a fire station forms mental images of what fire engines are like. If he has seen firemen fighting a fire, his concepts or visual images of fire engines are extended in that he knows how the equipment on the trucks is used. There are many valuable experiences which help your child develop concepts. As you go to the grocery store, hardware store, post office, bank, and garage, your child is learning the functions of these places. Special excursions like a trip to the zoo, police station, beach, junkyard, and vacations are valuable too. Many common experiences at home, such as working in the yard, helping you in the kitchen, and watching television, will help your child form concepts and thus he will be able to create many visual images when he reads.

19ab. *Seeing Relationships*. Help your child see relationships among objects by pointing out similarities and differences as you help him develop new concepts. For an example, you might say that chairs are to sit in, and files are used to store things. You can make up a little game of this activity by beginning a sentence and having your child finish it. Say, "Books are to read, pencils are to ...." Other examples are "Food is to eat, water is to ...." "We talk on the telephone, and .... television."

20a. *Find the Color*. Point out a color such as one that is found on a toy, wall, or other places in the house. Ask your child to see if he can find something else that is that same color. You can also extend your child's knowledge of colors by making a picture with him and pointing out what color you are using as well as what color he is using at the time. Later, when your child is reading stories which include the names of colors, he will be able to form appropriate mental pictures.

21ab. *One of These Things Is Not Like the Others*. Show your child different objects, three of which are related and one which is different. For example, you could show him a pencil, crayon, paint brush, and doll. Sing the *Sesame Street* version of "One of These Things Is Not Like the Others" or simply have your child point to the one that is different. By playing this little game, you will be helping your child see similarities and differences in objects which will, in turn, help him see relationships among ideas as he reads. Reading is a thinking process and requires the reader to organize and analyze the information he is gathering.

22ab. *My Picture Books*. Old catalogues with pictures are useful! Children love to cut out pictures and this aids hand-eye motor coordination. After your child has cut out many different pictures he can classify or group them together. For example, he might classify pictures according to toys, foods, things that make noise, or things that belong in a certain part of the house, such as the garage, kitchen, or bedroom. A separate picture book can be made for each classification. This activity helps your child organize his concepts.

23ab. *As Many as You Can*. Say some word and have your child tell as many words as he can think of to go with your word. For example, if you say food, he might say cereal, meat, apples, potato chips, and peanut butter. Mention some items in the category which your child has not mentioned. This activity helps your child classify the concepts he is forming.

24ab. *Riddles.* Riddles can also be used to extend concepts because characteristics of the objects are usually mentioned in the riddles. Say to your child, "I have a blade and wheels and make yards look nice. What am I?" Riddles are useful "time fillers" when you are riding in the car or waiting for something.

25ab. *Charades.* Whisper the name of an animal to your child and have him pretend to be that animal until someone else in the family guesses what he is. The child's concepts will expand as he sees others act out different animals, too. Children generally enjoy these family-type activities and learn much that will help them academically. This activity can be extended by having members of the family pantomime some common events such as talking on the telephone, brushing teeth, ironing clothes, driving a car, or eating different types of foods. Again, the child can guess what is being dramatized and of course take his turn in acting too.

26a. *Feel Me!* Put objects of different textures into a bag and ask your child to reach in and describe them without looking. He might say something is smooth, soft, hard, rough, or sharp. Some items you may want to use are cotton balls, sandpaper, wax paper, and different types of cloth. Of course take advantage of the natural opportunities to help your child learn about different textures as you examine new objects together. Have your child feel the objects and then tell him the word which is used to describe that texture.

27a. *Heavy and Light.* As you are doing things with your child, have him tell you what things are heavy and light. This will help him develop the concepts of descriptive words. You also might point out things that are big and little, bright and dull, rough and smooth, and cold and hot. You can help your child learn opposites by comparing and contrasting objects in his environment. Of course this activity will help your child increase his vocabulary, too.

28a. *Water Play.* Children can learn so much during bath time if you provide many different "toys" for water play. Different size plastic bottles help your child develop concepts of size and volume as he pours the contents of one into another. Your child will also learn more about weight as he observes that different objects float, while others sink. Many times children cannot verbalize what they are learning, yet learning is taking place.

29a. *How Many?* There are many opportunities when you can count with your child. As you are counting, your child is developing concepts of what different numbers represent. Of course you can count toes, the number of M & Ms he eats, the number of leaves he may be helping you pick up from the ground, or the number of forks you are putting on the table. Later when your child is reading words which represent numerals, he will be able to visualize how many things are represented.

30a. *Silly Sentences.* Tell your child you are going to say two sentences. Say one which makes sense and another one which is silly. For example, you might say, "Hamburgers are good to eat. Houses are good to eat." He can laugh to tell you which one is silly. Your child will be learning more about the characteristics of different objects while he is having fun identifying the silly sentence.

*31abc. *Vicarious Experiences.* Picture books are so valuable for providing experiences the child would not otherwise have. As you select books at the store or library, look for picture books which include pictures of things or places which your child cannot enjoy in person. Often pictures in the daily newspaper show places or things which your child may not be able to see or experience. The importance of looking carefully at pictures cannot be overemphasized. However, make sure you do not do too much talking. Point out one or two significant features and then wait for your child to ask more questions.

32ab. *Telling Stories.* As children listen to stories, they are associating their visual images with the words they hear. Telling your child stories enables him to use the concepts he is developing. Often, "story time" is a favorite part of the day for a child. You can use this time to the best advantage if you tell stories with many details. Of course in doing so you will be increasing your child's listening vocabulary as well as expanding his concepts.

Visual Skills

33ab. *Puzzles.* Puzzles are excellent training for visual discrimination. Commercial puzzles are good, but you can make your own by gluing a picture on a stiff piece of posterboard or cardboard and cutting it into pieces. As your child becomes more skillful in putting the puzzle together, cut the picture into more parts to make it more challenging. Your child can help you make puzzles, since it does not matter where they are cut.

*34ab. *Commercial Games.* Card games such as "Old Maid" and "Go Fish" require children to match pairs, so they are useful as a visual discrimination activity. Commercial picture lotto games also provide opportunities to practice this skill. As you select games and toys for your child, think what educational advantages they might have.

35a. *Cookie Cutters.* Children enjoy making different shapes using cookie cutters and play dough. Provide different cutters so your child will be able to see differences in shapes. Some of the plastic alphabet letters can also be used as cookie cutters. If so, have your child cut various letters and then put them on the table. Direct him to find the ones that are alike.

36ab. *Sticker Books.* Some of the simple commercial sticker books are easy enough for preschool children to do; however, many are too difficult. Children must make fine visual discriminations as they match the right stickers to the appropriate places in the books. Children generally enjoy this activity and at the same time are learning to look carefully to notice the differences in shapes. Of course this skill of visual discrimination is also necessary later as children discriminate different letters.

*37a. *Shopping Trips.* Once in a while it is a great experience for your child to go shopping with you. Many opportunities are provided for visual discrimination as you select the foods you need. Your child can help find his favorite cereal, special drink, and so forth. In doing so, the child is making visual discriminations and actually begins to feel that he can read. As you pass favorite places along the way, praise your child for noticing them. The importance of developing a positive self-concept at an early age cannot be overemphasized.

38ab. *Find the Hidden Pictures.* Visual discrimination pictures in *Highlights* and *Humpty Dumpty* magazines are valuable for visual discrimination, since the child is directed to find certain things. The addresses to these magazines as well as others can be found in Appendix D. I highly recommend that you begin subscribing to magazines during your child's preschool years.

39a. *Treasure Hunt.* You will need to have some plastic alphabet letter or letters on index cards for this activity. Lay them out on the table or floor and mix them up. Write a letter on a piece of paper and direct your child to find the letter in the pile that looks like the one you wrote. You can make this game exciting by using an egg timer or watch to see how quickly the child can find the missing letter. Of course your child will want his turn at designating a letter for you to find. If so, outline the letter with dotted lines and then have your child connect the dots to complete the letter. He will feel the differences in letters as he traces them.

40a. *Can You Find a* ————? Ask your child to look through a magazine article or on a cereal box to find a certain word or letter. For example, you may ask him to find the word "the" on a cereal box during breakfast. Make sure you write the word or letter for him so he can find the one that is like yours.

41a. *Which One Is Gone?* Display two or three alphabet letters on the floor or table and point out the names of each one to your child. Ask him to close his eyes or cover his eyes with his hand as you remove one of the letters. See if he can tell you which one is missing. If your child does not know the names of letters yet, you may use two or three different objects with which the child is familiar. Of course the child will want his turn at hiding one of the objects for you to guess which one is missing.

42a. *Looking and Seeing.* You can help your child notice more by asking him questions about what he has seen. For example, when your child is out of the room, ask him what color the walls are. You may also ask what is sitting on top of the dresser, or what pictures are hanging on the walls. Many children look but really do not see or notice the details. As you are talking with your child you will be increasing his vocabulary and concepts too. I hope you are beginning to see how the different readiness skills are related. Remember, they are only separated in this chapter for emphasis.

43ab. *Concentration.* The popular game "Concentration" helps children increase their visual memory. Duplicate cards from games such as "Old Maid" can be used. You can make your own pairs of cards with numbers, letters, or seals. To play the game, place all of the cards face down on the table and have each player turn two cards up. If the two cards match, the player can keep them and gets another turn. If the cards do not match, he turns them over again. Then the next person has a turn. Visual memory is required because the players must try to remember where different cards are located.

44a. *Making Patterns.* Ask your child to string beads or build block formations just like yours. Your child must look at your patterns carefully and make his exactly the same. Both visual memory and visual motor coordination are developed with this activity.

45a. *Drawing Circles.* Draw a big circle on your child's chalkboard or on a large piece of paper. Ask your child to make as many circles on your circle as he can without lifting his chalk or pencil. You can also have him connect different dots without lifting his pencil or chalk.

46a. *Clothes Pins.* Remember the old game of dropping clothes pins into a milk bottle? This develops eye-hand coordination! Pre-school children can play this game if you use the bottom half of a plastic milk carton.

47a. *Balance Beam.* Children can develop motor coordination by learning to balance on a walk or a curb, or you can easily make a balance beam. You just need one 2 x 4 10 feet long and three 2 x 4's about one and a half feet long. Use the three small 2 x 4's as braces. Cut notches in them so the long 2 x 4 (beam) can be held. For young children cut the notches two inches deep and four inches wide so the 2 x 4 will lie flat. When your child is skillful in walking the balance beam, make the notches 4 inches deep and 2 inches wide so he will be walking on the narrow side of the 2 x 4. Ask him to focus on a target at his eye level as he walks across the beam with heel touching toe. He can also learn to walk backwards.

48a. *Cutting.* Using scissors helps young children develop visual motor coordination. Have your child cut out pictures from old magazines or catalogues. He may want to make a little booklet of things that he likes. Later on you can label the objects and this will, in turn, help your child develop interest in words.

49a. *Bunting.* Staple a string or yarn to a rubber ball and suspend it from a doorway or rafters in the garage so it hangs at your child's chest level. Bunt the ball back and forth using wooden rolling pins or small bats. See how many times the two of you can hit the ball without missing.

50a. *Bean Bags.* Make a bean bag for your child by filling and stitching an old washcloth or some other material. Direct your child to throw the beanbag into an empty wastepaper basket. Increase the distance from the wastebasket to the child as he develops more skill. You can also have fun playing catch with the bean bag. This aids in developing eye-hand coordination.

*51a. *My Favorite Letters.* When your child learns to read his name, the letters in his name will probably be his favorite letters. As you are driving in the car, watching television, or eating breakfast, have him locate his favorite letters on the written materials that he sees. Tell your child some of your favorite letters (the letters in your name) so he will be able to make even more discriminations.

52a. *Is This Your Name?* Use plastic alphabet letters to form your child's name. Put your hand over your child's eyes and rearrange the letters. Then have him look at the letters carefully to see which ones have been rearranged. In addition to helping your child develop visual memory, he will be learning to read his own name.

*53a. *The Pointing E.* A pointing E game has been developed which parents can use with their children to detect eye defects in 3 to 6 year olds. This game is especially valuable for identifying a visual defect known as the lazy eye. Since one in twenty children in the 3 to 6-year-old age group has a visual defect, it is important for you to observe your child's visual habits. Parents are encouraged to send for the free *Pointing E Charts* which are available from the National Society for the Prevention of Blindness (NSPB). The address is: NSPB Home Eye Test, 79 Madison Avenue, New York, New York 10016.

Auditory Skills

*54abc. *Say It Clearly.* Many times children pronounce words incorrectly because they have heard them spoken incorrectly. Often as adults we become sloppy in our speaking habits without realizing the influence we have on our children. As you talk with your child and repeat words that he is learning, say them clearly so the child hears them correctly. In doing so, say new words slowly so your child can watch the formation of your mouth.

55a. *Hide and Find.* Hide a small object for the child to find. When he gets close to the object, clap your hands loudly. When he moves away from it, clap softly. Your child must listen to the clues in order to find the object.

56a. *Nursery Rhymes.* Capitalize on the fact that young children enjoy nursery rhymes. After reading a familiar rhyme to your child, pick out a couplet and read it again. Have your child supply the missing word. For example, you might say, "Little Bo Peep has lost her —————." Stories such as "Chicken Licken" and the Dr. Seuss book, "Hop on Pop" include many rhyming words too.

57a. *I Am Thinking of a Word.* Ask your child to think of a word that rhymes with your word. Any words may be used but a few suggestions are given below. Be sure the child knows what the word rhyme means.

a. I am thinking of a word that rhymes with red. You sleep in it.
b. I am thinking of a word that rhymes with mouse. We live in it.
c. I am thinking of a word that rhymes with tie. You like to eat it for dessert.
d. I am thinking of a word that rhymes with cat. You can hit a ball with it.

e. I am thinking of a word that rhymes with light. You can fly it.

f. I am thinking of a word that rhymes with toad. Cars go on it.

g. I am thinking of a word that rhymes with dish. They swim.

*58abc. *Guess What I Am Doing?* Have your child close his eyes while you make some kind of a noise. For example, you might be opening a bag of pretzels, using the can opener, getting silverware out to set the table, or tapping on the kitchen counter. You can help your child develop his auditory sense if you make him aware of the different sounds that are around us. This activity can be expanded later on if you simply sit and listen to the sounds. Keep in mind, however, that you do not have to be sitting to enjoy the sounds around you. If you are shopping in the downtown area, ask your child to listen to certain sounds of the city. Again you will be developing concepts as well as expanding his auditory sense.

59a. *Same—Different.* Say two words that are similar in sound and ask your child if you are saying the same word twice or two different words. For example, you might say bed and bid; bed, bad; can, hat; fat, fall; boy, toy; and dad, bad. Make sure your child is not watching your mouth for clues. The game is fun if you give your child an opportunity to say words and have you tell whether he is saying the same word twice or two different words.

60a. *Which One Does Not Rhyme?* This is another activity that is a good time filler and at the same time a valuable activity for developing auditory discrimination. Tell your child you are going to say four words. All the words should rhyme except one. Ask him to point out the one that does not rhyme. It will be necessary to repeat your four words at least twice. For example, you might say: write, fight, light, and see. The child should tell you that see is the word that does not rhyme.

61a. *Rhyming Nonsense Words.* As you are working around the house, substitute rhyming nonsense words for some common words. For example, as you go to the refrigerator to get the cheese, you might say, "I need a little sneeze." Other possibilities are lurkey for turkey, pilk for milk, hop for pop, and so forth. In addition to sharing a joke with your child, he will be learning to discriminate words.

62a. *My Telephone Number.* One meaningful way to work on auditory memory is to teach your child his telephone number. Teach him the first three numbers first. When he can repeat these, teach him the next four numbers. Sometimes singing the numbers is helpful.

63a. *Records and Songs.* Songs are helpful for building auditory memory. "Old MacDonald Had a Farm" is a good example since the child must repeat the different sounds of the animals throughout the song. Children do love music and can learn so much through it.

64a. *Say It Again.* Stories such as "The Old Lady and the Pig" and "The House that Jack Built" include many repetitions. Children generally enjoy hearing the words again and again. Ask your child to repeat the events or say them with you as you read the story.

Set aside a quiet time every day during which even the very young child can enjoy reading and looking at pictures.

65ab. *Let's Pack.* Start this game by saying, "I'm going to take a trip and I will take my toothbrush." Your child should then say, "I'm going to take a trip and I will take my toothbrush and toothpaste." With each turn repeat all articles which have been named and add one of your own. This game can also be played as grocery store. Say, "I went to the grocery store and bought some apples." The child repeats this and adds another article. This activity can help your child remember more and more words.

66a. *What Would You Like?* Allow your child to play waitress or waiter as you pretend to order food. Begin by responding with one or two items which you would like and continue increasing these as the child's auditory memory increases. You can vary this game by having your child pretend to be a clerk as you order groceries.

67ab. *Telephone.* You can have fun with the entire family by playing telephone. To begin the activity, one person whispers something to the child. The child whispers it to the next person, who whispers it to the one beside him, until it reaches the last person. It is always fun to hear the outcome.

68ab. *Can You Remember?* When giving directions to your child, begin by including only one action. For example, you might say, "Will you please put the napkins on the table." As your child's auditory memory increases, increase the number of directions given at one time. For example, you might say, "Please put the napkins and silverware on the table." Praise your child for a job well done. Keep in mind that sometimes children who have an excellent auditory memory, may only hear those things that they want to hear.

Interest in Words and Books

69a. *My Name Is.* The most important word to any child is his name. You can teach your child his name by writing it on belongings such as books and toys. Simply putting a name tag on his door will make him feel special and can also help him learn his name. For anyone handy with a jigsaw, a puzzle with your child's name would be worth the time and effort.

70a. *Tell Me About This Picture.* Children love to look at photographs. Ask your child what he sees in the picture and then write what he says below it. He will be learning that the symbols actually represent words if you read what he says again. Later the child will probably be asking you what the words say or he will be "reading them to you." This activity helps children realize that reading is talk written down.

*71ab. *Mail.* Children love to receive their own mail! Encourage grandparents, aunts, uncles, and other relatives and friends to send little notes or letters to your child. The child will begin to develop the desire to read his own notes.

*72ab. *Reading Signs and Labels.* As you travel around your neighborhood and community, you will see thousands of signs. Read some of them aloud or say, "I wonder what that sign up ahead says?" Similarly, children generally enjoy the pictures or special offers that are made on the backs of cereal boxes. If you read some of these offers, your child will develop interest in words.

*73abc. *Subscribe to Children's Magazines.* Many birthday and holiday presents are broken before the special day is over, but for a fairly reasonable price you can get your child a magazine subscription that will last throughout the year. Most of the magazines for preschool and elementary school children include many reading activities in addition to good stories. *Humpty Dumpty, Jack and Jill, Wee Wisdom,* and *Highlights* are favorites of young children. Names and addresses can be found in Appendix D.

*74abc. *Develop the Library Habit.* Take advantage of the library story hours, book clubs, and little plays, in addition to checking out books for your child and yourself. Ask the children's librarian what books and activities she recommends most highly for your child.

75a. *Watch Sesame Street.* Nearly seven million children watch *Sesame Street!* Results show that children who watch this program are learning. The goals of the program are clearly outlined and include most of the readiness skills. Do not expect *Sesame Street* to do the entire job, but capitalize on the actions and characters which fascinate children.

76a. *Use Post Cards and Pamphlets.* When you visit a special place, have your child select some inexpensive post cards of his favorite scene. As tells you about the pictures, write down what he says and read it back to him. You can make little books by pasting the pictures on paper. The free pamphlets that most children take usually have good pictures and can be used for this activity too.

77a. *Assembling Pictures.* Give your child pictures of some activity that shows a story in sequence. Most comic strips are good for this if they only have three or four parts. Have the child assemble the pictures and make sure he puts the first picture on the left. An example of a picture story is provided here. This activity will help your child develop left to right progression.

78a. *Label Objects.* Perhaps the most effective way to help children develop left to right progression is to have them watch as you are writing words. You can label objects in your child's room or other parts of the house. In doing so, write the letters about 2 to 4 inches tall and use the Guide for Printing letters which follows. Have your child watch and listen as you write the word and say it. Then have your child place the word in front of the object which is on the card. If you want to see if your child can match the words with the objects, have him collect all the cards, shuffle them, and then ask him to place them where they belong. Do this only when your child is beginning to show interest in words.

79a. *Coloring Books.* Coloring books with words accompanying each picture are good learning aids. As your child is coloring the picture, tell him what each word says. Later you might want to have him cut out both words and pictures and match them.

*80ab. *Write a Book.* One of the best ways to help your child develop interest in books is to write a simple story about him or some experience he has had. The following procedures can be used. First talk about something. You may want to review what you did on a particular day or the fun that you had on a recent outing or trip. The child might also talk about things that he likes, such as his pets, toys, or daily activities.

After talking with your child, tell him this would make a good story and then ask how to begin the story or simply write a sentence which he has used. Be sure to use big print on the typewriter so the writing is clear. Have your child notice that you are going from left to right as you are writing the words. Usually two or three sentences are sufficient. Here is an example of a story a four-year-old boy dictated: "There are four people and one dog in our family. Our dog is named Disney. We go grocery shopping and play ball."

After you have written your child's story, read it to him. In doing so, point to the words so he sees you are moving from left to right. Of course the child will also notice that reading is talk written down. This is why it is so important for you to use the exact words that your child says.

This method can be expanded by putting the stories in book form. Children love to make "All About Me" books. For example, one page of a book could be used to tell about members of the family, another for favorite games, and one for favorite foods. Other possible topics for the one-page stories are: my pets, my best friends, my favorite television programs, or what I like to do on Saturday. Of course you do not make the book at one sitting, but rather as the child becomes interested.

If you want to make this book very attractive and one of which the child will be especially proud, you can make a hard cover for it. Suggestions are presented by Janice Gross in Appendix B. Your child will be very proud of his efforts and will enjoy showing others his book or books.

*81abc. *Continue Reading Those Stories.* I believe the most valuable way that you can help your child desire to learn to read is that of reading stories to him. Children soon discover there are many adventures in books which cannot be found on television and are available at times when the television programs are not. In addition, books have the advantage of being able to be read again and again and again. Some stories your child will want to hear many times. By reading to your child, you are helping him value reading and books. Save time for this very important activity. In addition to getting books from the library, buy some books for your child so he can begin his personal library. Perhaps the

Guide for Printing Letters

Use this guide when you write letters or words for your young child.

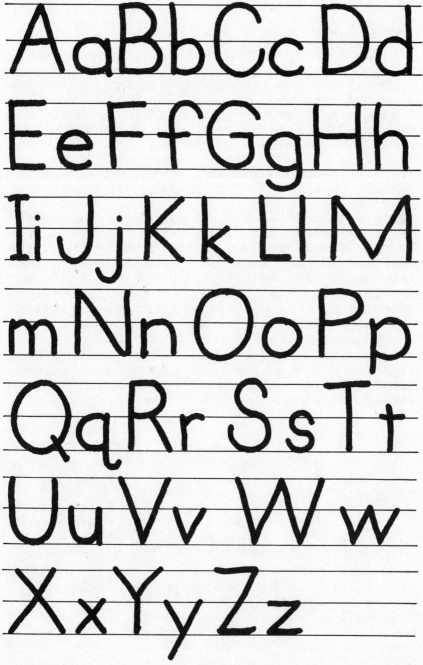

best source of suggestions is the buyer for the children's books at your favorite book store. They know the books which are best sellers and for which ages they are appropriate.

Names of Letters

82a. *Now I've Said My ABC's.* Children generally enjoy the alphabet song; however, being able to sing it does not guarantee that a child knows the names of letters. Some children say, "L-M-N-O-P" as if it were some kind of word As your child is singing the alphabet song, have him point to each letter as he says it. Simply write the letters in a row, allowing enough space between each letter so the child can point to each one separately. An example follows:

a b c d e f g   h i j k l m n o p
q r s t u v   w x y   z

83ab. *As You Are Traveling.* Ask your child to look for certain letters as you are riding in the car. Begin with letters that he knows and that appear frequently such as a, e, s, t, and r. If your child knows alphabetical order, play a game in which a is found first, b second, and so forth.

84a. *Loading the Truck.* Plastic alphabet letters can be used in so many ways to teach letter recognition. There are trucks available with plastic letters, or, use any dump truck and a set of plastic alphabet letters. As you help your child load the truck, ask for certain letters. If the child does not know the letter, show him and have him trace its shape.

85ab. *Alphabet Book.* Your child can make his own alphabet book or letter book by cutting out pictures and pasting them on paper or posterboard. You can label the pictures with both capital and small letters. Some easily pictured words are:

A — apple	J — jacks	S — sun
B — boat	K — kite	T — top
C — cat	L — lamp	U — umbrella
D — duck	M—mouse	V — vest
E — egg	N — nest	W — wagon
F — fish	O — octopus	X — xylophone
G — goat	P — pail	Y — yard
H — house	Q—queen	Z — zebra
I — ice cream	R — rake	

86. *Name That Tune!* If you have a toy piano or a xylophone, label the keys which represent a to g. This can be done by using a cardboard keyboard or actually writing the letters on the keys with a water-soluble magic marker. Direct your child to strike the following letters in sequence: ccggaag-ffeeddc. The result will be a familiar song (*Twinkle,*

Twinkle, Little Star). A child will be able to enjoy music as he is learning the names of the letters from a to g.

87a. *At the Beach.* Children generally love to play in the sand. After building a few castles, write some letters in the sand and have your child name them. Allow him to make some letters for you to guess also. Tracing the letters in sand helps reinforce the shapes of the letters.

88a. *Scratch My Back.* Form a letter on your child's back by tracing with your index finger. Children enjoy having their parents touch them so they will enjoy guessing the letters you are making in addition to feeling loved.

89ab. *Clay Letters.* Your child can make letters by forming them from clay. In addition to seeing the letters, he is able to feel them. Pipe cleaners can also be formed into letters and glued to cardboard, but this requires more parental aid. These activities are especially appropriate for letters that are easily confused such as o and c, m and w, b and d, and u and n. Write the letter clearly so the child can form it with the clay or pipe cleaner.

90a. *Fishing for Letters.* When your child is having a bath let him play with some of the letters from the set of plastic alphabet letters. He can "fish" by finding a letter and naming it. If he is able to name the letter, he keeps it. If he does not know the name of the letter, tell him, and then put it back into the water. See how many "fish" he can catch.

91a. *Spotty.* Draw a simple outline of a dog on a piece of paper and write various letters your child is learning on the dog. Tell your child the dog's name is Spotty, so he needs spots instead of letters. Give your child a crayon and direct him to name each letter. As he names the letter, he can color it with a spot. Go over any letters your child does not know by drawing them on a large piece of paper and asking your child to trace them. At the most, work on only two letters at one time.

92a. *Words I Can Spell.* The most meaningful way to help your child learn the names of letters is to teach him to spell words which are of interest to him. Most children want to be able to spell their own name, mommy, daddy, their pet's name, and perhaps their siblings' names. Upon request write these words for your child and then spell them by pointing to each letter in the word.

CHAPTER THREE

HELPING YOUR CHILD USE PHONICS

There is probably nothing in reading instruction that is desired by parents more than phonics instruction. Yet, it is the area of reading instruction that is most perplexing to parents. Many parents want to be able to help their child use phonics, but they do not understand how to go about it. This chapter includes a description of the elements of phonics, guidelines for helping your child use phonics, and many ideas and games that you can use in working with your child. In addition, Appendix F has many words and generalizations concerning particular sounds which will aid you further as you help your child. The suggestions concerning phonics are divided into four categories: consonant sounds, vowel sounds, sound patterns, and dividing multi-syllable words into syllables so phonics can be applied.

The Elements of Phonics

Consonant sounds make up 24 of the 44 sounds in the English language.* All of the consonant letters except c, q, and x record at least one distinct sound. In addition, some consonants are combined together to form a new speech sound (ch, sh, *th,* th, ng, and wh). Key words for the 24 consonant sounds are listed below:

b as in baby	ch as in chin	d as in did
g as in go	h as in hat	j as in job
l as in little	m as in mom	n as in not
r as in rat	s as in see	sh as in shell
wh as in whale	y as in yard	v as in vase
f as in fit	z as in zoo	k as in kind
p as in paper	t as in tie	w as in was
th as in thin	*th* as in then	ng as in ring
(voiceless)	(voiced)	

*There is disagreement concerning the number of sounds in the English language. The 44 sounds which seem to appear most frequently are included in this chapter. You may want to talk with your child's teacher to see if there are other sounds your child is expected to learn.

In addition to the 24 consonant sounds, children learn that some consonant sounds blend together to make one sound. A consonant blend is not a new sound, but rather a blending of the sounds of two or more consonants. Some common consonant blends are listed below along with sample words:

Two-letter blends

sc as in scooter	sk as in skates	sm as in smoke
sn as in snail	sp as in spider	st as in stick
sw as in swing	bl as in blocks	cl as in clown
fl as in flower	gl as in glove	pl as in plate
sl as in sled	br as in bread	cr as in crown
dr as in drum	fr as in frog	gr as in grapes
tr as in train	pr as in present	

Three-letter consonant blends

sch as in school	spl as in splash	scr as in screen
spr as in sprinkler	str as in straw	thr as in three

Teachers generally teach the consonant sounds first because the consonant sounds usually appear first in words and are more consistent. Also, many teachers feel consonants are more important than vowels. See if you can read the following sentence with some of the letters left out.

-i- a-- -e--y -e-- -o --e -a--.

Now try the sentence

J-m -nd J-nn- w-nt t- th- p-rk.

As you see, all of the consonant sounds were excluded from the first sentence, and only consonant sounds were included in the second. This example shows you just how important consonants are.

The consonants b, h, j, l, m, t, p, v, r, and d are generally taught first because they only have one sound. After children can identify consonants at the beginning of words, instruction is directed towards learning consonant sounds in the final and then medial positions.

The *vowels,* a, e, i, o, u, and sometimes y, represent 20 different sounds in the English language. A list of the most frequently accepted vowels along with key words follow:

a	e
short a as in apple	short e as in let
long a as in ate	long e as in eat
â as in care	ê as in hear, irrigate
ä as in car	er as in her, first, and burn

i
short i as in it
long i as in bite

o	u
short o as in lot	short u as in up
long o as in go	long u as in use
ô as in or or horn	
oo as in tool	
oŏ as in book	
oi as in oil, and boy	
ou as in out, and cow	

The schwa sound as
    a in ago
    e as in agent
    i as in sanity
    o as in comply
    u as in focus

You will notice the vowels have a long sound which sounds like their names. There are also short vowel sounds such as in the words: Fat Ed is not up. Sometimes two vowels glide together to produce a new sound which is called a diphthong (oi as in oil and boy, and ou as in out or cow). All vowels can make the schwa sound which is the vowel sound in an unaccented syllable. Notice the double oo's (tool and book) make new vowel sounds as do all vowels which precede the letter r (car, care, hear, irrigate, her, first, burn, and or). As you can guess, vowels usually are more difficult for children to learn since only a few letters represent so many different sounds. Again you are referred to Appendix F for many sample words concerning each one of these sounds.

In addition to learning the consonant and vowel sounds which are a part of the English language, children learn many generalizations or rules to help them know when certain letters have certain sounds. The major generalizations concerning the consonant sounds and vowel sounds are also presented in Appendix F.

There are some sounds in the English language which appear together so frequently they are called *sound patterns*. For example, "all" is found in ball, call, fall, hall, mall, tall, and wall. Other common word families are am, an, at, old, ad, it, ake, ay, en, ent, ill, ell, and et. If your child knows the consonant sounds and the sounds of these sound patterns, he can make hundreds of words, so it is wise to teach children these common sound patterns. Sample words which can be formed with consonants and these sound patterns can be found in Appendix F.

The last component of phonics which is considered in this chapter is *syllabication and accent*. It is necessary to consider syllabication as a part of phonics because before a child can sound out a multi-syllable word, he must divide it into syllables. He will also need to know which syllables are accented or sound louder so he can pronounce the word correctly. The most important generalizations concerning syllabication and accenting which your child is expected to learn are also found in Appendix F.

Most of the elements of phonics are taught in the kindergarten, first, second, and third grades, and then reviewed in the intermediate grades. Again, the activities in this chapter are classified according to the level (a, b, or c) at which they are usually emphasized; however, children do differ in phonics instruction. If your child has experienced difficulty with phonics, do not criticize him, but rather accept him as he is. It might be valuable to review the general guidelines for helping your child which were presented in Chapter One. In addition to the general guidelines, the following will help.

Specific Guidelines to Follow in Helping Your Child Use Phonics

Some reading specialists and programs believe many sounds should be taught before children learn to read words. I disagree. Talk with your child's teacher to determine whether she first teaches sounds *or* a few words by sight. Follow her suggestions. If she says sounds, use the ideas in the first part of this chapter. If she says words, you can use the ideas in the first part of Chapter Four initially.

a. Before a child begins to work on phonics he should have a large listening vocabulary and be able to see and hear differences in letters and sounds. Activities for these skills were suggested in Chapter Two. Your child will not be successful in accomplishing the activities in this chapter unless he has the prerequisite auditory and visual skills. Similarly, if your child is able to sound out a word, this skill does not do him much good unless the word is a part of his listening vocabulary. For example, if your child can sound out the word "mandatory," and yet has never heard anyone use this word, the phonetic analysis is useless.

b. Most children should learn a few words by sight before you attempt to help with phonics. Words are more meaningful to children than letters and sounds and if the child knows some words, you will be proceeding from the known or concrete to the unknown or abstract. For example, you would be wise to teach your child the word "boy" before trying to teach him the sound of /b/. The letter "b" does not have any meaning, whereas, the word "boy" does. When your child knows the word "boy" or as you are teaching it to him, you can help him see that the first sound is /b/. If your child does not know any words at this time, you may want to read the first section of Chapter Four which deals with sight words. I believe your child should know many of the words on "Forgan's Initial 101 Sight Word List" before attempting phonics instruction.

c. About 85 percent of the words in the English language are phonetic. Some words such as "one" must be learned with other word recognition techniques as suggested in Chapter Four. Phonics is not the total answer for success in reading.

d. Remember that reading is a process of getting meaning from printed symbols — not just pronouncing words. As you work on phonics make sure you are stressing meaning too. To be able to pronounce the word "mall" is worthless unless the child has a concept of what mall means.

e. Do not make your child memorize rules for the vowel sounds, dividing words into syllables, and so forth. The important thing is that he be able to apply the rules when he is sounding out words. In general it is agreed that the best procedure for helping a child apply rules is to direct him to discover or see the rule. Specific examples of how to do this are included in this chapter.

f. On helping your child sound out a word, do not ask him with what letter the word begins, but rather ask him what sound is at the beginning. Knowing that the word bed begins with the letter b does not help you pronounce it. However, knowing that it has the /b/ sound at the beginning is very helpful. If you ask your child what sound a word has at the beginning, and he tells you the name of the letter, simply ask him what sound that letter has.

g. Do not have your child break words into each independent sound, but rather emphasize sound units. For example, in trying to say the word basket, the child should pronounce bas/ket rather than b-a-s-k-e-t.

h. Before a child can sound out a word that has more than one syllable or sound unit, he must divide the word into syllables. You would be wise to use only one-syllable words with beginners in phonics instruction. You will notice nearly all of the words in Appendix F are one-syllable words.

i. After your child has acquired some efficiency in analyzing words phonetically, it may still be desirable to tell him some words. Stopping to sound out every word may seriously interfere with comprehension and in what should be a pleasurable process of getting meaning. In such cases a sensible parent supplies the word so the child may get on with the story. If necessary you may want to review the word and its sounds later.

j. Your child must learn to develop a procedure for sounding out words. Too often these sounds and principles or generalizations concerning them are taught in isolation and children have a difficult time "putting it all together" to pronounce unfamiliar words. It will be necessary to talk with your child and list the steps he can follow to figure out unfamiliar words. A suggested procedure is included in the last activity of this chapter.

You are ready to begin helping your child use phonics *if* he does know some sight words. As mentioned earlier, if your child does not know any words at all, you would be wise to begin with the first part of Chapter Four which includes suggestions for helping your child learn some basic words by sight. After doing so, or if your child already knows some words by sight, you will find suggestions for helping your child learn about consonants, sound patterns, vowel sounds, and syllabication and accent in this chapter.

Consonant Sounds and Generalizations

93a. *I Spy.* Begin this game by saying the beginning sound of something that you spy in the room. For example, you might say, "I spy something that starts with /m/." Remember to say the sound rather than the letter. Ask your child to look for something in the room that begins with that sound. After he guesses the correct item, he can have the next turn.

94ab. *Particular Sounds.* Teach particular consonant sounds by referring to the appropriate list in Appendix F for words that begin with that sound. Have your child say them after you pronounce them. Ask him how all the words are alike. Help him see that the words sound alike at the beginning. Point to the letter and repeat the sound. Make sure your child looks at the letter carefully so he can begin to associate it with the particular sound. Tell him if he wants to read a word he does not know, he can say the sounds.

95ab. *Toss the Block.* You can use small building blocks that have letters for this game. Ask your child to toss the block on the floor and give a word beginning with the letter that is on top of the block. If he hesitates, provide clues by describing some objects that begin with the letter.

96a. *Leaving on a Jet Plane.* Begin this activity by saying a sentence that includes the name of a place where you are going. The child is to make another sentence by naming things he would like to take with him. The first letter of each item must *begin with the same sound* as the place you named. Some examples are:

   a. "I'm going to Maine and I will take some meat." Your child can continue this by adding "money, medicine, marbles, and mother."
   b. "I'm going hunting and I shall take a horse." Your child might add, "hat and hamburger."
   c. "I'm going to Florida and I will take some flowers." Words such as "flag, flippers, and flies," or other words that begin with the fl blend might be used in responding.
   d. "I am going to the beach." Your child might say, "I will take a boat, bat, ball, and bucket."

97a. *Pot of Gold.* Place plastic letters which represent some consonant sounds on the floor in an arc approximately one foot apart. At the end of the letters put a surprise (Pot of Gold). This may be a piece of candy or some other treat for your child. Direct him to say the sounds of each consonant as he picks them up. He gets a reward when he can name all of the sounds on the way to the Pot of Gold. Only use a few sounds at first so the child will be successful. If he says a sound incorrectly, tell him the sound and read sample words from the appropriate list in Appendix F.

98ab. *Book of Blends.* Write the name of a blend at the top of a piece of paper. Give your child old magazines to find pictures which begin with that consonant blend. Direct him to cut out the pictures and glue them on to the appropriate page. Add other pages as your child learns more blends. If you keep them in loose-leaf form you can use them to play some of the games in this section. Again you might want to check Appendix F for sample words.

99ab. *What's a Word?* Make a set of cards by writing a consonant sound or a consonant blend on each one. Place the cards face down on the table. Ask your child to draw a card and name a word beginning with the same letter or blend. Now it is your turn. If the drawer cannot name a word within ten seconds, he puts the card back. The winner is the person who has the greatest number of cards after the entire pile has been exhausted. Do not hesitate to make an error occasionally to see if your child catches it, but emphasize the correct sounds.

100ab. *Tic-Tac-Toe.* Print symbols of sounds in the tic-tac-toe squares. Play the game by making x's and o's in spaces as usual, but you and your child must say the sound before using the space. A variation is to have your child say a word beginning or ending with that particular sound.

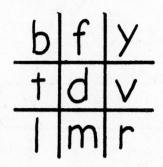

*101ab. *All Around Us.* There are many opportunities for helping your child learn the consonant sounds. For example, as you help him clean his room you may say /ch/ is for chair, /b/ is for basket, /p/ is for pants, and /dr/ is for dresser. This way your child will have many opportunities to hear the beginning sounds isolated, and before long will be telling you the beginning sounds of common objects.

102ab. *Junk Drawers.* Children generally enjoy exploring the items in junk drawers. As your child takes out an item, ask him for another word beginning with the same sound. Continue until all of the objects are out of the drawer.

103b. *Discover.* To help your child learn whether the sound c is pronounced /k/ or /s/ have him listen as you read the following list of words. Tell him to notice the sound at the beginning.

cap	cut	cot	cent	cider
cat	cub	cop	cellar	city
cell	cup	come	circle	cycle

After reading the words, ask him what sounds c has at the beginning. Then have him look at the letter that follows the first sound. See if he notices that when c is followed by e, i, or y, the sound of c is usually /s/. When c is followed by a, o, or u, the c usually has the /k/ sound. Use nonsense words such as cer, cur, and cor, to see if your child is able to apply the generalization to unfamiliar words.

104ab. *Electric Company. Electric Company* is a television program which is similar to *Sesame Street* in that it is designed to teach certain reading skills. It is different from *Sesame Street* in that it deals with higher level reading skills. Occasionally watch the program with your child and you will learn many ideas for helping him.

105ab. *Race Track.* Draw an oval which represents a race track on a sheet of paper. Make approximately 15 lines to divide the race track into sections. Print a consonant sound in each section. Have your child roll dice or spin a spinner with numbers to see how many sections he can move. He then moves his marker the number of spaces indicated. In order to stay on that space he must say the sound printed on it and give a word containing that sound. If he is wrong, he moves back until he lands on a space containing a sound he can say. Keep taking turns until a player reaches the finish line. You may want to refer to Appendix F for sample words which begin with a particular sound.

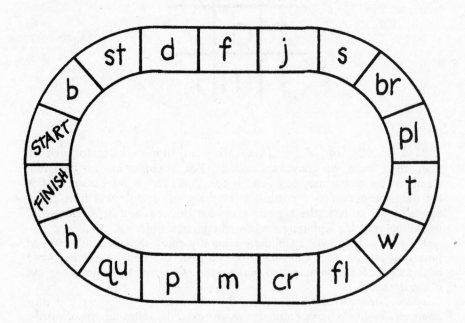

106ab. *Alphabet Foods*. Children generally enjoy the cereals, soups, and macaroni products that contain letters of the alphabet. You can take advantage of teachable moments by telling your child to find certain letters to make a word, or by suggesting words for him to form.

*107abc. *How Do You Spell ———?* As your child develops an interest in writing words, he will be asking you how to spell different words. Sometimes simply respond by telling him the letters. Other times, repeat the word and say, "What sound does it have at the beginning?" If your child is able, also help him to hear the other sounds in the middle and the ending of the word. This activity will help your child develop more independence in spelling because you are teaching him to listen to the sounds and think of the letters which represent the sounds.

108ab. *Buddies*. You can help your child realize some consonants blend together to produce one sound by telling him some letters are buddies. "Buddies" say one sound by putting their separate sounds together. Give him some examples by writing some of the words found in the word list in Appendix F. Ask him to find some of the words in his favorite books. It will take many repetitions with words before your child realizes which letters often appear together and make certain sounds.

*109abc. *How Was School Today?* When your child comes home from school take time to talk together as he enjoys a snack. Look at his papers to see the kinds of things he is learning. Often you can reinforce what he has learned by reading the papers orally and providing praise for doing a nice job. At the same time, help your child realize he cannot always get everything correct. Respond to incorrect items by saying, "that was a tough one" or "let's see if I can figure this one out — it is a hard one." Perhaps you can play games such as tic-tac-toe or some other activity suggested in this chapter by using the items which are on his school papers. Some reading programs are beginning to include practice sheets for parents to use with their child. If you are fortunate enough to have these, use them!

Sound Patterns

110a. *Words I Know*. Your child's reading vocabulary can increase rapidly if he knows many of the consonant sounds and sound patterns. You can help him realize how many words he can read by making a little booklet which includes one page for each sound pattern. For example, on one page of the booklet you could write "an" and then list all of the words that your child knows that have the an sound pattern (perhaps can, fan, man, pan, ran, and van). In addition to including words with sound patterns, include some of the words that your child may have learned by sight. You may want to cover this booklet with a hard cover because it will be one of which the child is very proud. See Appendix B for suggestions for making hard covers for books.

111a. *Pick Up Patterns*. Print some of the sound patterns on small cards. Place them face down on the floor. Ask your child to turn one up at a time and say the sound of the pattern. He gets to keep the card if he is correct; you get it if he is incorrect. Teach one pattern at a time by saying the sound and words that have that pattern.

112ab. *Any Sound.* Make a deck of 40 cards using the words which are suggested for sound patterns found in Appendix F. Also make 5 cards with "any sound" written on them. Shuffle the cards and deal 5 to each player. The player to the left of the dealer plays any one of his cards, reading it as he lays it down. The next player plays a card that either rhymes or begins with the same sound as the first card. For example, if "call" has been played, the word "ball" which rhymes with call or can which has the same beginning sound could be played. If a player cannot play, he draws from the pile in the center until he can play or has drawn three cards. If he has a card with "any sound" written on it, he may play this card and name a word that can be played upon it. The first player who uses all of his cards wins the game.

113a. *What Word Is the Truck Carrying?* Make a simple truck and write a sound pattern on it. Also make a strip of paper with consonants to pull through the opening as shown in the illustration. Direct your child to pull the strip down and read each new word as it appears to find out what the truck is carrying.

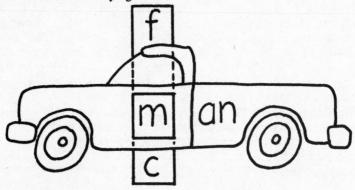

114ab. *Spill and Spell.* Buy blocks with different letters of the alphabet on them and put them in a container such as a plastic milk bottle. Have the child spill the blocks from the container and, without turning any blocks over, let him make as many words as he can with the letters shown. Count one point for one-letter words, two points for two-letter words, three points for three-letter words, and so forth. Remember to time with a timer. Your child will soon learn that he can form many words by using sound patterns.

115ab. *Solitaire.* You will need to make two equal decks of cards for this game. One deck should include only cards with consonants and others should contain sound patterns. Place both decks side by side. Have your child turn up one card from each deck. If he makes a word, he can keep the cards. If he cannot make a word, he must discard those cards in a separate pile and turn up two more cards. He should continue playing until both decks are exhausted. He can count the number of cards which form words and compare this number with the next time he plays.

*116ab. *What's This Word?* When your child is reading and encounters an unfamiliar word ask him if he sees any familiar sound patterns. Often children can pronounce a word that appears difficult if they analyze it. Point out the sound pattern by covering other letters. Encourage your child to look at the beginning and ending sounds, too.

117ab. *New Words.* You will need 3 x 5 and 5 x 8 index cards for this activity. Staple the 5-inch side of several 3 x 5 cards to the 5-inch side of one 5 x 8 card. Write a beginning sound on each one of the 3 x 5 cards and a sound pattern on the 5 x 8 card. Ask your child to say the sound pattern and then to pronounce the words which appear when he turns the different consonant sounds. Your child may enjoy making these cards. Sample words for the most common sound patterns are found in Appendix F.

118ab. *Cycling.* Make a bicycle path on a piece of paper. Divide the path into sections and write a common sound pattern on each section. Ask your child to listen as you "ride the bike" or to read the sound patterns he knows. If he says a sound pattern correctly, he has traveled one mile. See how many miles he can travel.

This game can be varied if you suggest a consonant and tell your child to see how many words he can make during his bicycle ride. If your child happens to say a word that he does not understand, provide a simple explanation. For example, if the child combines /b/ and /an/ to form the word "ban" you might say, "They ban burning leaves in our city. That means they stop us from burning leaves in our city."

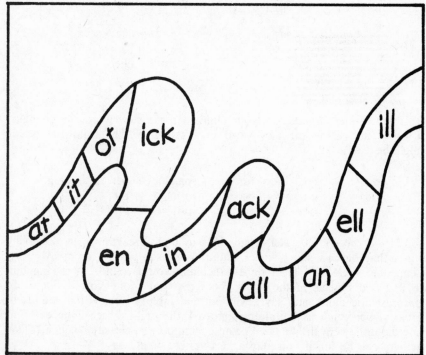

Vowel Sounds and Generalizations

119ab. *Old Maid*. Make a pack of 40 word cards using the following words plus one "old maid." This game is played like *Old Maid* except books are made out of two cards with the same vowel sound. First, deal all cards one at a time to each player until the pack is depleted. Each player removes all pairs of cards from his hand. As he does this, he states the vowel sound his pair represents, reads the words, and lays the cards down. To begin play, the dealer allows the player at his left to draw one card from his hand. The player puts down any pair he may have formed by the card drawn and then allows the player to his left to draw a card from his hand. This game continues until all cards have been paired except one — the old maid. The player with the old maid loses. Use the following words for the 40 word cards.

Long a Sound	Short a Sound	Long e Sound	Short e Sound
play	hand	keep	let
say	mat	feet	bed
late	lap	bead	red
tape	pan	cream	pet

Long i Sound	Short i Sound	Long o Sound	Short o Sound
ice	it	boat	got
pie	bit	go	hot
bite	did	no	clock
kite	fit	road	top

Long u Sound	Short u Sound
suit	us
use	bug
Sue	rug
cute	truck

120ab. *Quiet Game*. Ask your child to make new words by changing a vowel and using the new word in a sentence. The following words might be used:

bit	cot	fur	pan	pet	big
b-t	c-t	f-r	p-n	p-t	b-g
b-t	c-t	f-r	p-n	p-t	b-g

121b. *Vowel Hunt*. Ask your child to find three things in the living room that have a short vowel sound. For example, he may say, "rŭg, lămp, and window." Then review the long vowel sounds by asking him to find two objects in the living room that have long vowel sounds. In this case the child may say, "windōw and tāble." Review the sounds of other vowels such as diphthongs and ask the child to see if he can find any diphthongs in the house. For an example he might say, "couch." This activity can be fun if you play it in a variety of places.

122b. *Guess My Word*. Say, "My word begins with the blend br, it ends with the /k/ sound, and the vowel sound is a long a. Guess my word." The child then tries to say the word. Pronounce it for him if he is incorrect. Allow him to give you the next word.

123b. *Exercises*. Ask your child to stand with his arms folded across his chest. When you say a word with a short vowel sound he should drop his arms to his sides. When you say a word with a long vowel sound he should raise his arms above his head. If you say a word that has a vowel sound which is neither long or short, he should put his arms straight up. Sample words for the vowel sounds can be found in the word list in Appendix F.

124b. *Cross Out*. Ask your child to cross out the vowel that he does not hear in each of the following words. Later, he can read them to you saying the long vowel sound in each word. See if he can state the generalization, or rule, for double vowels. He should realize the first vowel is long and the other one is silent.

toad	tail	weak
beat	speak	meal
toast	pail	eat
coat	maid	chain
meat	leaf	cream

125b. *Magical E*. Index cards are needed for this game. On the front of each card write a word that can be changed by adding the letter "e" to the end of it. On the back of the card, write the letter "e". When the card is folded the e should touch the base word. Let your child practice making new words by adding the "Magical E." Words you might use are: pin (e), hat (e), hid (e), rid (e), rat (e), cut (e), past (e), and plan (e). Have your child notice the vowel sound is short without the final e and is long with the final silent e.

126b. *Open and Closed*. Have your child discover that a vowel is usually long in a syllable (open) that ends in a vowel, and usually short (closed) in one that ends in a consonant. Ask him to read words to see if the vowel sounds are long or short. Give him clues to help him notice why the vowel is long or short. The following words might be used for open syllables:

Open	*Closed*
no	pot
we	wet
me	set
$\bar{\text{va}}$/$\bar{\text{ca}}$/tion	bid
$\bar{\text{ti}}$/ger	hid
$\bar{\text{mo}}$/tel	had

Ask your child to see if he can find any examples of open and closed syllables in some of his books or magazines.

*127ab. *Commercial Games.* There are many commercial games available concerning phonics. Some suggested materials which are readily available at many toy stores can be found in Appendix E.

128b. *Bossy R.* You can help your child see how bossy the letter "r" is by making a large capital R on a piece of paper. Divide the R into sections, as illustrated below, and then write start, finish, and words from the list in Appendix F in which the vowel precedes the letter "r". Direct your child to throw a die or spin a spinner to see how many spaces he can move. To be able to move his token he must be able to pronounce all the words along the way and indicate what the vowel sound is. Now it is your turn. The first one to the finish line is the winner.

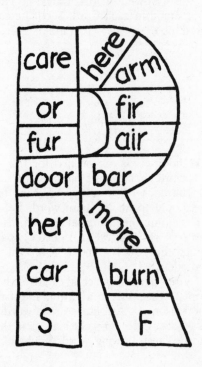

129b. *Generalizations Everywhere!* List many words that apply to a certain generalization. For example, you may list words which have two vowels together, in which the first vowel has a long sound and the other one is silent: meat, beat, boat, soak, clean, sleep, cream, rain, and main. Read the words and ask your child to notice how they are alike. Also have him look at the words. If he does not see that the two vowels appeared together ask him, "What do you notice about the vowels in the word?" If he still does not see this, tell him that the two vowels are together.

Read the words again and ask him to listen carefully to the vowel sound that he heard in each word. In doing so, exaggerate the long vowel sound so that he is sure to hear it. Also point out that the second vowel is not heard.

Have your child think of some other words that apply to this generalization, by having him find words in his books or magazines. Caution your child to remember that generalizations concerning vowel sounds do not always work, but they are worth a try to see if the vowel should be pronounced using the long or short sound.

Syllabication and Accent

130ab. *How Many?* Before your child will be able to divide words into syllables, he must be able to hear the different syllables in a word. Ask him to clap once for every syllable you say as you pronounce some words. For example, when you say "basketball," he should clap three times. Children need to realize that a syllable is a sound unit which is composed of one or more sounds blended together. If your child has difficulty with the above game it may be that he believes every sound in a word is a syllable.

131bc. *Syllable Puzzles.* Write 10 two- or three-syllable words on index cards. Cut the index cards apart at different angles between the syllables in each word. Mix the word parts and have your child fit the words together and pronounce the words.

*132bc. *Listen to the Sounds.* Help your child divide words into syllables by directing him to listen to the last sound in each syllable and the first sound in each syllable. Many times children cannot verbalize a rule or generalization for dividing words into syllables, but can successfully divide the words into syllables if they listen to the sounds. Of course this habit will also help your child as he spells words.

133bc. *Syllable Math.* You can make math problems for your child by writing words and then having him add the number of syllables. This is a good time filler when waiting for someone or riding in a car. In addition, your child will have some practice in dividing words into syllables. Some examples follow:

basketball (3)	underwater (4)	desk (1)
any (2)	medicine (3)	telephone (3)
goal (1)	swimming (2)	lamp (1)
+ helper (2)	+ bucket (2)	+ calendar (3)

134bc. *Because.* Make a list of words which follow a particular rule for syllabication. Have your child read the words or look at them as you read. Ask him to draw a line between the syllables and finish the statement "I divided it here because —————." Some words which include double consonants which are preceded and followed by a vowel are: supper, timber, ribbon, number, ladder, master, cargo, donkey, and tablet. Your child should divide these words between the double consonants and say he divided them there because we usually divide words between double consonants if a vowel precedes and follows the double consonants.

135b. *Hit the Table.* Ask you child to listen to a word you pronounce to hear which syllable sounds louder. The second time you say the word he should tap on the table when he hears the accented syllable. Some possible words are: invitation, sailboat, vacation, and football.

*136bc. *Look It Up!* Help your child apply what he is learning by looking up words in the dictionary to notice the accent marks. Explain there may be a primary and secondary accent mark. Ask him to notice the difference in the two marks. You may tell him the primary accent mark is darker. Explain that the primary accent mark tells him to say that syllable louder than any other syllable in the word. Look first at words he knows and then have him try out his skills by reading words that are unfamiliar.

*137bc. *What Should You Do?* It is important for children to realize the steps they can use to sound out words. Ask your child what he should do when he tries to sound out a word. He may say:

a. Divide it into syllables if it is more than one syllable.
b. See if the syllables are open or closed.
c. Look for other clues to the sounds: sound patterns, bossy r, or diphthongs.
d. Pronounce each syllable.
e. Say the word.

FOUR OTHER WAYS TO HELP YOUR CHILD RECOGNIZE WORDS

In addition to phonics, there are four other techniques which your child can use to recognize words and it would be most desirable if he could employ all five techniques. Your goal is not only to aid him in phonics, but also to help him (a) learn many words by sight so he does not have to labor over every word, (b) look for prefixes, suffixes, or other structural clues in words, (c) use context clues by skipping the unknown word and trying to figure it out by reading the rest of the sentence or paragraph, and (d) use the dictionary to check the pronunciation and meaning of new words.

Word recognition is most efficient when the child can use a combination of techniques. For example, if your child is stumped by the word "lubrication," he might use the principles of phonics to divide the word into syllables and sound it out. He may skip the word and read the rest of the sentence to get some idea of the meaning of the word. He may be able to notice the "tion" ending of the word and realize that "tion" is pronounced "shun." To do so, he had to memorize that "tion" does not sound as it is spelled. This is really sight recognition. Finally, your child may need to use the dictionary to determine the pronunciation and/or meaning of the word. As was mentioned earlier, phonics is not the total answer to success in reading. Children need to learn a variety of word recognition techniques.

There are *some words that your child should learn by sight*. Listed below are 101 words that are probably the most important for your child to learn initially in developing his reading vocabulary.

I developed Forgan's Initial 101 Sight Word List by considering (a) what words are important to children, (b) what words appear most frequently in writing, and (c) by considering the 44 sounds in the English language. As you read the list of words, you may notice that these are words that appear frequently and that each one of the 44 sounds in the English language is represented. I highly recommend that these be the first 101 words that your child learns to read. Sample sentences and stories in which these 101 words are used can be found in Appendix G. Keep in mind these are only sample sentences and stories. You will be able to write others which are more appropriate for your child.

Forgan's Initial 101 Sight Word List

Nouns and Pronouns

mommy	they
daddy	boy
sister (or sister's name)	girl
brother (or brother's name)	me
pet (or pet's name)	there
child's name	them
friend (or friend's name)	you
(name of favorite toy)	we
(name of favorite food)	it
(name of favorite place)	I
	he
	she

Adjectives and Adverbs

(child's favorite color)	new
this	all
the	which
a	their
your	soon
one	that
good	as
my	some
when	then
our	very
his	not
her	

Prepositions and Conjunctions

to	on	and
in	out	but
for	of	about
at	from	so
with	by	it
or	it	up

Verbs

was	is	take
come	like	eat
get	can	give
think	am	saw
look	are	came
run	have	could
would	see	said
do	will	went
make	be	did
work	has	jump
play	been	bring
were	go	use
		had

These words are arranged according to the part of speech in which they are normally used, so a sentence can be formed early. Keep in mind some of the words can be used as more than one part of speech.

As mentioned earlier, I believe most children should learn some words by sight before instruction in phonics is begun. Many reading programs begin by teaching some basic sight words to the children, and then have the children analyze the sounds as a way of developing knowledge of phonics. There are some other children who learn best by beginning to learn the sounds in the language and then putting these sounds together to form words. Their sight vocabularies are actually developed by many repetitions with the words they have learned by putting sounds together. You should talk with your child's teacher to determine what approach she is using with your child. If the teacher is teaching the sounds first, and then having the children synthesize the sounds to form words, you should follow the suggestions in Chapter Three first.

Conversely, if your child's teacher is teaching some of the basic sight words before attempting any instruction in phonics, you should read the suggestions in the first part of this chapter. Later your child will analyze the sounds which are in different words as a way of helping himself learn the sounds. Both approaches to phonics instruction have been found useful with different children. Observe your child to see how he is responding to the approach which is being used; however, do not change your approach without first talking to your child's teacher.

Regardless of which approach is taken to initial reading instruction, there are some words that your child must learn by sight. As mentioned, approximately 85 percent of the words in the English language follow the principles of phonics. There are some words and some parts of words which must be memorized because they do not follow phonics. The old argument of the phonic method versus the sight method is no longer an issue. Reading specialists and teachers realize that both are needed for successful reading.

Another technique that will help your child figure out some words is that of noticing *the structure of the word*. Often a prefix, suffix, or two words combined together such as in a compound word, make words look unfamiliar to children. For example, your child may know the word "happy," but if the prefix "un" is added, it may at first seem unfamiliar to him. Your child should learn to look at words that are more than one syllable to see if they include prefixes, suffixes, or if they are compound words. As a part of learning about the structure of words, your child will also be learning to pay attention to apostrophes. Your child will soon learn that apostrophes are used in contractions and are also used to indicate possession. Again it may seem uncanny to us, but a child may have a difficult time recognizing a familiar word if there is an apostrophe s to indicate possession. He needs to learn to be aware of these structural elements.

Your child will learn that a prefix is a separate syllable at the beginning of a word that changes the meaning of the root word. A suffix is a separate syllable at the end of a word that modifies the meaning of the root word. Some of the most frequently used prefixes and suffixes are as follows:

Common Prefixes and Suffixes

Prefixes	Meaning	Sample Word
ab	from, away	absent
be	by	beside
com	with	compile
de	from	depart
dis	apart, not	disbelief
en	in, into	encircle
ex	out of, from	exit
in	into, not	insecure
pre	before	preview
pro	in front of, toward	project
re	back	rebound
sub	under	submarine
un	not	unhappy
able	that can be	portable
ance	act of	disturbance
ant	one who	assistant
ence	state of being	indifference
ent	one who	president
ful	capable of being	hopeful
less	without	painless
ment	state or quality of being	amazement

Suffixes	Meaning	Sample Word
ness	state or quality of being	kindness
ship	office, status of, rank of	assistantship
tion	act, state or condition	action
ward	tending or leading to	homeward
s	plural	works
ing	the act of	working
ed	past tense	worked
er	noun, used to compare	worker
est	used in comparing	latest
y	adjective	dirty
ly	adverb	slowly
ies	plural	ladies
es	plural	glasses

Sometimes it is possible to figure out the pronunciation and meaning of a word by its location in the *context*. Perhaps you have skipped an unfamiliar word when reading and then looked back at it to consider its meaning in relation to the other words in the sentence or paragraph. This is called "using context clues." Context clues are usually used in combination with other methods of word identification. For example, if a child does not know the word "bananas" in the sentence, "I like to eat bananas," he must still look at the sounds of the word to figure out what it is. From the context he knows the word represents something edible; now he must look at the sounds to see exactly what it is. Context clues enable the child to make an educated guess rather than simply guessing wildly or skipping the unknown word.

At the beginning levels of reading instruction, picture clues are sometimes taught along with context clues. That is, the child is encouraged to look at the picture to determine the unknown word. If the child is reading the sentence, "I like to eat bananas," but does not know the word "banana," he can look at the picture to see what is being eaten. Of course when a picture is not included or if a picture illustrates something else, the child cannot rely on picture clues; thus, this is not emphasized as a technique of word recognition.

Another method of figuring out unfamiliar words is to look them up in a *dictionary* or *glossary*. This technique is very useful to find the pronunciation of words that cannot be determined with other methods. Children should learn that re-spellings of words are usually included in parentheses after the main entry in a dictionary and a pronunciation key is included on each pair of pages in a dictionary. A child can look at the re-spelling and use the pronunciation key as a guide to the sounds in the words. Of course the dictionary is an excellent source for discovering the meanings of words too.

Picture dictionaries are used at the primary grade levels before children learn the many skills that are required to use a regular elementary school dictionary. Some of the most popular picture dictionaries and elementary school dictionaries are listed in Appendix H, along with other reference books for elementary school children. Talk with the person who purchases the children's books at your local book store to determine which one is most appropriate for your child's abilities at this time. Keep in mind that your child will probably have many dictionaries throughout his school years, since his skills and needs change. Do not buy one which, though excellent, is too difficult for your child.

As simple as using a dictionary may seem to us as adults, there are actually many skills involved. Children must be able to locate the word by opening the appropriate section of the dictionary. Usually children are taught to think of the dictionary in quarters. The a through d words are found in the first quarter, the e through l words are found in the second quarter, the m through r words are found in the third quarter, and the s through z words are found in the last quarter. Knowledge of alphabetical order and skill in using guide words are also necessary. Once a child finds a word, he must be able to use the pronunciation key and select the appropriate meaning. In doing so, he usually encounters many abbreviations. Using a dictionary is not an easy task! Your child will need your guidance.

Sight Words

138a. *Making Cards.* A meaningful way to help your child learn some of the initial sight words is to have him make cards for a friend or relative. Of course in doing so, he will be using many of the words that are on the 101 initial sight word list. Have him tell you what he wants to say and you do the writing. After writing the words, read them to him and ask him if there are any words that he knows. Read the sentences again and then have him read them. Keep in mind that many repetitions are required for a child to learn a word by sight.

*139a. *Using a Word List.* The initial 101 sight word list which was presented earlier in this chapter can be very valuable if used correctly. Keep in mind that it will be impossible for your child to learn all 101 words at one time. Also, since many of the words are prepositions and conjunctions, they must be used in meaningful sentences. Do not have your child simply memorize this list of words. Since you will be using the words often, I suggest getting a package of 3 x 5 index cards and writing each word on a separate card. You will be able to use these frequently and also your child can use the word cards to make sentences. First choose four or five of the words which make a meaningful sentence. You might put the words in order so they form a sentence such as, "Mommy and daddy like me," and read this sentence to your child. In doing so, point to each word. After you have read the sentence several times, see if the child can find the word "mommy." Continue this procedure with the other words. Finally, mix the five cards and give them to the child and see if he can put them in order to form the sentence. Have him look carefully at the letters which make up a word which is difficult for him. Refer to Appendix G for other sample sentences and stories in which the 101 words are used.

140a. *Hurdles.* Place some of the word cards on the floor in a row. Ask your child to read the words as quickly as possible. If he reads the word correctly he has jumped the hurdle and can continue by reading the next word. If he misses a word, read it to him and ask him to begin again. Time him to see how quickly he can "jump the hurdles."

141a. *Buying Balloons.* For this activity have your child cut some circles. Write one of the basic 101 initial sight words on each circle. Tell your child that the circles represent balloons and he can "buy a balloon" by reading the word. See how many balloons your child can buy. You can vary this activity by drawing a tree with branches and placing round word cards on the tree. Tell your child these are apples and you want to see how many apples he can pick by reading each word. If there are words that your child is having difficulty learning, have him look at them carefully and use the word in a sentence to make sure he understands the meaning. Perhaps tracing each letter in the word while he says the word will help him remember it.

142a. *Hide and Seek.* Hide cards with the words the child is learning in various parts of the room. Ask the child to find them and as he finds them have him read them. Keep a record of how many cards the child is able to find and read, and then compare this to the score he receives the next time you play the game.

143ab. *Trace Me.* If your child cannot read a word by just examining it carefully and learning it after several repetitions, ask him to write it. The writing should take place after the child knows the meaning of the word and has formed a visual image of it. He can study the word and then write it without looking at it. Compare the copy to the original word to see if it is written correctly. If not, the child should study the word again, say it, and attempt to reproduce it from memory.

If he still does not remember the word, you might try the kinesthetic or tactile approach. Another sense — that of touch — is employed in this method.

   a. Ask your child to use the word in a sentence or to give the meaning of it.

   b. Say the word and write it with a crayon on a separate piece of paper, using letters that are at least 2 inches high. As you write the word, say each syllable as it is written. When the word is completed, say it again.

   c. Demonstrate the tracing technique while the child watches. The child may trace the word with his index finger, index finger and second finger, or thumb and index finger. Have him first say the complete word. As he traces ask him to say each syllable rather than saying each letter of the word. When he has completed tracing the word, ask him to pronounce it again.

d. Check your child's tracing technique. When he hesitates or makes an error, stop him. Have him begin again and praise him when he succeeds.

e. Remove the copy of the word the child has traced and have him write the word on a fresh piece of paper when he feels that he can reproduce it from memory. Always have him write from memory, rather than simply copying the word.

f. Check the writing of the word to make sure it is correct. If the child hesitates or is not able to write the word from memory, have him retrace the word as a whole. Do not permit him to erase in order to correct errors, but rather have him retrace the word. Continue this procedure until the child is able to reproduce the word from memory.

g. The final step is to have your child find this word in a book or a magazine. This will help him transfer his knowledge of the word to the actual reading situation.

As you can see, this method is very time-consuming. Use it only if your child is having difficulty learning some particular words. Discontinue the use of this method if your child is frustrated and makes many errors. Consult Chapter 10 for further suggestions if your child is not progressing as well as expected.

144ab. *Sad Face.* Use a deck of 50 cards from the 101 initial sight word list. The deck should also include 5 cards with a sad face drawn on them. Place the deck face down on the table. Have your child begin by turning up a card, pronouncing the word, and placing it in a pile in front of him. He continues until he misses a word or draws a sad face. The object is to correctly pronounce as many words as possible before drawing a sad face or missing a word. Record one point for each consecutive word pronounced correctly. Shuffle the cards and begin again to try to better the previous score.

145ab. *How Many Sentences Can You Make?* You will need all of the 101 words from the initial sight word list for this activity. Give them to your child and ask him to see how many sentences he can make using the words. You can make this activity more exciting if you set a time limit, for example 5 minutes. This activity can also be varied by asking your child to see how long a sentence he can make. Again, a time limit may be valuable. Sample sentences of varying lengths can be found in Appendix G.

146ab. *Auto Racing.* Make an auto racing course by drawing a track and dividing it into squares of equal size. Use a toy racing car to mark his progress as the child moves around the track. Direct him to turn up a card which has on it a word from one of the 101 initial sight word list. If he pronounces it correctly, he moves his racing car one square closer to the finish line. If he is unable to say the word within 10 seconds, tell him the word, and have him say it and then move his car. Time your child to see how quickly he can move around the track. Keep records of the times on different days to see if your child can improve his speed.

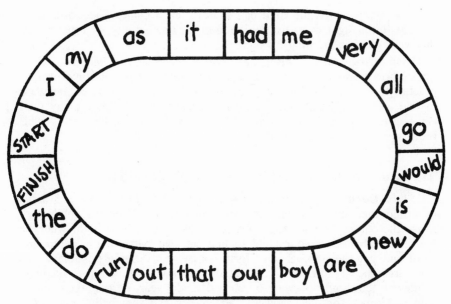

147ab. *Golfing.* Make 9 packs of 3 cards each with words from the 101 initial sight word list. Each pack of cards represents one of the 9 holes on a golf course. Shuffle the cards and have your child put the pack for the first hole face down on the table. Ask him to turn each card over in turn, try to pronounce it within 3 seconds, and then go on to the next word. Every time he pronounces a word correctly, a mark is made on a score card. The number he gets right on the first hole (first pack of cards) is his score for that hole. Notice the number he gets correct is counted as his score, since children generally like to get the highest rather than the lowest score possible. Continue in this manner with the 9 packs of word cards. Keep a chart record of scores so the child can see his progress. Also, make a note of the words he is missing and have him look at the words carefully and trace them as he says the word. As your child learns more words, increase the number of words in each pack (hole).

148ab. *How Many Words Can You Make?* Provide your child with several plastic alphabet letters or letters that you have written on index cards. Ask him to see how many words he can make using the letters. Time limits such as 5 to 10 minutes make this activity enjoyable. The activity is also more exciting if you take a turn at making some words. In doing so, you may want to introduce some new words to your child.

149ab. *Word Baseball.* To play this game, designate one corner of a room as home plate and the other three corners as first, second, and third base. You can be the pitcher by flashing sight words to your child. If he pronounces a word correctly within three seconds, he may go to first base. If he says the next word, he may go to second base, on the next turn he goes to third base, and then scores a home run when he gets the fourth word correct. If he is unable to pronounce a word, he is out and then goes back to bat again. The game is over after 3 outs. The object is to see how many runs your child can score in each game. The words from the 101 initial sight word list can be used for this activity, or other words that your child is learning by sight.

150ab. *How Many "The's" Can You Find?* You can help your child realize how frequently some words appear, and at the same time provide practice in identifying the words, by asking him to find a particular word in one of his books or magazines. For example, say, "How many the's can you find in this book?" Vary this activity by using other words. This is an especially good quiet activity.

The Structure of Words (Structural Analysis Skills)

151ab. *Compound Puzzles.* Write a compound word on a 3 x 5 index card and then cut between the two words which form the compound. Make the cut at such an angle that the child knows he is right when he puts it together. Ask your child to find the two parts of the compound word and put them together to form a new word. Some possible words are: fireman, grandmother, basketball, playhouse, horseshoe, flagman, gentlemen, cowboy, doorway, overboard, underwear, earthquake, candlestick, salesman, football, sidewalk, watchman, and snowball.

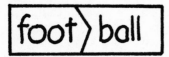   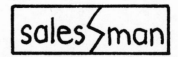

152ab. *Compound Words.* The same puzzle pieces which you used to make the above activity can be used to play this game. Shuffle the cards and deal two cards to each player. Place the other cards face down on the center of the table. The object of the game is to make as many pairs as possible by getting both parts of the compound word. The first player asks the others for a particular word that goes with one he has. If a player has it, he must give it to the one who asks. If no one has it, the asking player draws a card from the deck. Now it is the next player's turn. Continue until one player forms three compound words.

153ab. *Find the Endings.* You can call your child's attention to the endings of words by having him circle them. Give him a newspaper or take one of the stories from his magazines and ask him to circle all the "ed, ing, s, and ly" endings. Be specific, by saying, "Find the five *ing* endings in this column." This activity encourages your child to look at the endings of words and at words carefully when pronouncing them, rather than just guessing by looking at the beginnings of words.

154ab. *Add an Ending.* Make a list of several words on a piece of paper and ask your child to add an ending, such as s, er, ing, or ed. Ask him to use the newly formed words in a sentence. Have him point out how the endings change the meaning of words. For example:

$$work + er = worker$$
$$want + ed = wanted$$
$$jump + ing = jumping$$
$$eat + s = eats$$

155ab. *Look at My New Hairdo.* Discuss the fact with your child that many times people change a hairdo or some feature that makes them look different. They may not be recognized at first, but after looking carefully they will be recognized. Tell your child this can happen with some words. Sometimes there is a beginning or an ending added to the word that makes it look different, but if one looks carefully at the word and identifies what makes it look different (prefix, suffix), one may be able to recognize it. Provide practice by having your child find words in his magazines or books that have a prefix or suffix.

156b. *Who Is the Owner?* To help your child realize that an apostrophe can be used to show ownership, point out possessive words as you are reading. Tell your child that the apostrophe can show what somebody owns or has. Ask him what the person or thing possesses in each one of the examples you use with him. You can also develop this skill by giving your child a word with an apostrophe such as "dog's." Have him make a sentence showing what the dog owns or has.

157b. *Contraction Concentration.* To play this game you will need index cards. Write a contraction on one index card, and then make separate cards for each of the two words that make up that contraction. Do this for approximately ten contractions. Place the words face down on the table and then follow the regular rules of *Concentration* except that instead of turning up two cards, the player turns up three cards. The object of the game is to try to turn up the contraction, and also the two words that make up the contraction. If the person is successful in doing so, he gets to keep all three cards. If not, the cards are turned face down again and the next person gets a turn. Some contractions that you may want to use in making up this game are as follows: he's, can't, won't, aren't, I'm, don't, she's, you're, doesn't, and here's.

158ab. *Colors, Circles, and Lines.* Structural elements can be pointed out by marking the word parts in some distinctive way. For example, the words forming a compound word can be printed in two different colors, or the separate words can be circled or have a line drawn between them. Your child can then pronounce the new word as a whole. You may want to color the endings of some words that are giving the child difficulty (i.e., them and then). By making the word distinctive in some way to illustrate the structural element, you will be helping your child look carefully at the structure of words.

159b. *What Does "un" Mean?* As you are reading to your child or talking with him and come across a word that begins with the prefix "un", ask your child what the prefix means. If he does not realize that this makes the word mean the opposite, you can give him examples that are part of his listening vocabulary. For example, words such as unhappy, untie, undo, unfamiliar, unfair, unhealthy, unkind, unload, unlock, unnecessary, untouchable, unusual, and unwise are fairly common words. Use some of these words in sentences to help your child learn the meaning of un. In addition to recognizing prefixes and suffixes, your child needs to understand how they change the meanings of the words. You can do this with other prefixes and suffixes also.

*160ab. *What's This Word Again?* As your child is reading to you and makes a mistake by omitting the end of some word, simply pronounce the ending for him. After he has finished reading the story, go back to some of the words that he has missed, point out the endings, and ask him to say the words again. This will help your child look carefully at words rather than simply guessing at the first few letters.

Context Clues

161ab. *Splish.* As you are reading a story to your child, substitute the word "splish" for some word. Ask your child to guess what the "splish" word is. Talk about the fact that he usually has to hear the rest of the sentence before he knows what the word is. Similarly, when he encounters an unfamiliar word in reading, he should skip the word and read the rest of the sentence or paragraph, as this might give him the clue to the word. When your child is reading and comes to a word he does not know, remind him of this technique.

162a. *Picture Clues.* As mentioned earlier, children should not be taught to rely on picture clues; however, during initial reading instruction, pictures can be used to aid the child in pronouncing unknown words. Ask your child to look at the pictures before he reads so he can use picture clues along with other word recognition techniques. In addition to helping him pronounce the word, pictures can help the child understand the word better.

163bc. *Missing Words.* This is a quiet activity and requires that you prepare a series of sentences in which part of a word is missing. Ask your child to read the entire sentence and fill in the letters that are missing to form the missing word. Samples follow:

1. Farmers are interested in ag--c--t---.
2. The teacher was very ab--pt because she was angry.
3. He was im-ob-le so they called an ambulance.

164abc. *Cross Out!* You will need some of your child's magazines for this activity. Cross out every fifth or seventh word in the story or article. Ask your child to read the material and write in the word he thinks is missing. Check his responses with the correct words. For example:

Summer is ———— favorite season of the ————. Children do not have ———— go to school. Many ———— take vacations, too. Some

————go on picnics together. ——— to the beach is ——— too. September comes too soon ——— most children.

*165bc. *Guidance Helps.* As your child is reading and comes to a word he does not know, tell him to skip it and read the rest of the sentence to determine what it is. If he cannot, simply pronounce the word for him. If he says a word, but it is incorrect, have him look at the sounds of the word. One advantage of having your child read to you is that you can guide his development of the word recognition techniques. Remember not to become so involved in the recognition of words that you forget to see if your child is comprehending and enjoying the story. By suggesting techniques to your child, and praising him sincerely when he uses them, you will be helping him develop effective reading habits.

*166bc. *Types of Context Clues.* You can help your child understand there are a number of different types of context clues. He is not expected to memorize these; however, being aware of several kinds of context clues will enable him to become more adept in using them. For example, tell your child that sometimes he may be able to use a definition context clue. A sample sentence using a definition context clue is, "She *categorized* the foods by placing them in four basic food groups." In this sentence, the child can realize that categorizing has something to do with placing objects in groups.

A synonym context clue may also give your child some indication of a meaning of an unfamiliar word. In the sentence, "The boy was *frightened* and his dog was *scared* because they were lost," your child may be able to get the word "frightened" if he knows the word "scared" or vice-versa. In other words, sometimes synonyms are used in the same sentence and if your child knows one of the words, it may help him understand the meaning of the other word.

In the sentence, "He was *sad,* but she was *delighted,*" your child may be able to understand the word "delighted" by noting the contrast. Contrast clues are used frequently, and can be of value if your child knows the meaning of one of the contrasting words.

Sometimes a common saying or common expression is used in a sentence and can give the child a clue to the meaning of an unknown word. For example, in the sentence, "It was lucid and clear as a bell," the child may be able to recognize or understand the word "lucid" if he is aware of this common saying or expression.

Once in a while the mood or situation of the story will help the child understand a word which may appear unfamiliar. For example, in the sentence, "The teacher was *abrupt,* because she was *angry,*" the child may realize that one behavior which could go together with anger is abruptness.

Point out the different types of context clues in natural situations as you encounter them when you are reading or when your child is reading to you. Many examples will be necessary before your child will be able to recognize these automatically.

Dictionary Skills

167a. *Alphabet Puzzle*. Print the letters of the alphabet in proper sequence on a large piece of paper or cardboard. Then cut this into pieces to make a puzzle. Ask your child to put the puzzle together. As he becomes more skillful in putting the puzzle together, you can cut it into more pieces.

abc/def/ghij)klm/nop/qrst/uvwx/yz

168ab. *Plastic Letters*. You need to use plastic alphabet letters for this activity or make index cards with a separate letter of the alphabet on each card. Mix the 26 letters in a box and ask your child to put them in alphabetical order as quickly as he can. Time your child and compare his times on different days. At the beginning stages you may want to make another set of letters so the child can refer to these in placing letters in alphabetical order.

169ab. *Alphabet Hopscotch*. If your child enjoys playing hopscotch, and is having difficulty with some of the letters of the alphabet in terms of sequence, print these letters in sequence on the squares of a hopscotch diagram. As your child hops to each letter in alphabetical sequence, he should say the name of the letter. This game is particularly good for learning the more difficult parts of the alphabet, such as o, p, q, r, s, t, u, v, and w.

170ab. *Telephone Directory*. You can help your child make a "friend telephone directory" by compiling the names of friends and relatives. Have him list the names in alphabetical order according to last names. Show him your telephone directory and have him notice the guide words, the fact there are only a few names beginning with q and x, and that names beginning with the same letter are alphabetized by succeeding letters. Do not show too much at one time; watch the reactions of your child.

171ab. *Three in a Row*. Shuffle the alphabet index cards and deal five to each person. Place the remaining cards face down on the center of the table. The object of this game is to get three cards with letters that are in sequential order (c, d, e). The first player takes one card from the top of the stack. If he cannot use it, he discards it by placing it face down in the discard pile. If he can use it, he must discard another card from his hand so he never has more than five cards. The first player to get one book of three letters in sequence is the winner.

172bc. *Hidden Message*. Print a message for your child in which you use z for a, a for b, b for c, c for d, and so forth. Your child has to know what letter precedes another letter since the code uses the previous letter "a" to represent the letter "b". For example, see if your child can figure out this message:

Xnt bzm gzud z ohdbd ne bzmcx

173ab. *Goofy Letters.* Plastic alphabet letters or the alphabet index cards are needed for this game. Place the letters in alphabetical order to begin the activity. Ask your child to close his eyes as you change the sequence of a couple of letters. Then ask him to find the "goofy letters" and change them so they are in alphabetical order. Now it is your turn!

174bc. *Watch Me.* The idea of this game is to teach your child to alphabetize by the second, third, and fourth letters of words beginning with the same letter. Make some flash cards with words that your child knows or use flash cards that you have already made. Make sure you have words that begin with the same letters such as many, milk, make, meat, made, and mile. Place the cards in alphabetical sequence and ask your child what he notices about the order of the words. Give him an opportunity to discover the rationale, but if he does not see the words are alphabetized by the second, third, and fourth letters, tell him how you did it. Use a dictionary or telephone directory to show him that words are listed in this manner. Have him alphabetize some other flash cards with words that begin with the same letter so he can practice this skill.

175ab. *Before and After.* When you are riding in a car or waiting for someone to arrive, ask your child to tell you what letter comes before and what letter comes after the letter you give. For example, if you say w, the child should say v comes before it and x comes after it. He will want to have a turn, too.

176ab. *Picture Dictionary.* Your child can make his own picture dictionary by cutting out pictures that begin with the different letters of the alphabet. Get 26 pages of construction paper and label each one with a letter. Ask your child to draw or cut pictures beginning with each letter and paste them on the appropriate page. As your child is ready, you can expand his knowledge of the dictionary by writing guide words at the top of the pages, including a pronunciation key at the beginning, and listing multiple meanings of words. A picture dictionary is never complete.

*177bc. *Dictionary Dividers.* If your child's dictionary does not have a thumb index, you might be wise to write a to d on the binding of the words from a to d, e to l on the second quarter of the dictionary, m to r on the third quarter of the dictionary, and s to z on the last quarter of the dictionary. These letters generally are used in designating the four quarters of a dictionary. Give your child some words to look up and ask him to hold the dictionary so the side binding is down on the table and to notice the four quarters in looking for the words. It will not take him long to realize that opening the dictionary to the appropriate quarter helps in locating the word quickly. I realize that you may hesitate to write on your child's new dictionary, but remember, this will not ruin the dictionary and will help your child develop skill in locating words quickly. One

75

of the reasons that children fail to use the dictionary as a word recognition technique is that it requires so much time. Help your child develop skill in locating words quickly so looking a word up in the dictionary is not a burdensome activity.

*178bc. *Together.* When your child is first learning to use a dictionary, you should help him locate the words. In doing so, point out the guide words. Ask your child what the words are at the top of each page. If he is not sure, tell him to look at the first and last words on the page and then ask why these two words would be put at the top of each page of the dictionary. Help him realize these words guide the reader in locating a word and are therefore called guide words. Make a list of meaningful words for your child to find and have him use the guide words in locating them.

179bc. *Think and Write.* Write two guide words such as "desk" and "elephant" on a piece of paper. Give him a time limit and ask your child to list as many words as he can think of that would appear between these two guide words. Each correct word scores a point. For incorrect words, subtract one point from the score. This is a good quiet activity when you are on a long car ride. To make the activity more difficult, indicate two guide words which begin with the same letter, such as "matter" and "meter."

180bc. *Time Find.* You will need a timer for this game. Tell your child a word and have him locate it in the dictionary. See if he uses the quarters of the dictionary and guide words. Time him on the same words other days to see if he is getting faster. Compare the times when he uses the clues, such as a quarter of the dictionary and guide words, for locating words as compared to not using them.

*181bc. *Pronunciation Key.* Help your child learn to use the pronunciation key in his dictionary by showing him that it is usually included on each pair of pages in the dictionary. Find a word he already knows and look at the re-spelling of the word together. Then show him the key words for each sound in the pronunciation key. Then find a word that he does not know and ask him to use the pronunciation key to determine the correct pronunciation. Tell him the pronunciation key is very useful when there is no one around to tell him what the pronunciation of a difficult word might be. Give examples of how you use the pronunciation key. Your child will only use the pronunciation key if he sees the value of it.

182bc. *Which One Is Right?* Use a word which has multiple meanings in a sentence and ask your child to find the appropriate definition in his dictionary. Write the word so your child can find it quickly. After he locates it, show him the different definitions and help him select the appropriate one. Sample sentences are:

a. We have an *account* at that store.
b. The *console* was as beautiful as the music that came out of it.
c. The *lip* of the cup was cracked.
d. The baseball player ran to the *plate*.

Help him notice that he must listen to or read the sentence again so he will know how it is being used.

*183bc. *Keep Out.* Keep your dictionary in a place where it is very easy to use. Children learn many new words from listening to you and watching television. Help them develop the dictionary habit by saying, "Let's look up that word." You will be able to guide your child in applying the many skills which are required to use a dictionary. Of course, this is only possible if you keep the dictionary in a place where it is convenient to locate and use.

*184bc. *Glossaries.* Look at your child's textbooks to see if they include a glossary of specialized terms. Glossaries are generally found in health books, social studies books, science books, and in some math books. Point out the different features of the glossary as you look at it with your child. For example, you may show him the pronunciation key, guide words, re-spellings for proper nouns, and so forth. If your child is aware of the aids that are available to him in a textbook, he will be more likely to use them.

CHAPTER FIVE

HELPING YOUR CHILD COMPREHEND WHAT HE READS

Understanding the Comprehension Skills

Parents often say, "My child can read, but he does not understand what he reads." My response is that the child is not reading unless he comprehends — reading involves meaningful interpretation! Being able to pronounce or say words does not mean the child is comprehending. Understanding does not take place automatically. Thinking is required as the child relates the printed symbols to his oral language and background of experiences.

As your child reads the sentence, "Bobby, Beth, and Lynette were excited because they were going to go to Disney World," he must relate these words to his oral language. If he can recognize the words "excited," "going," and "Disney World," and has heard them used before, his chances of comprehending are better. Also, if he can relate these to the experience he has had when feeling excited, going places, and perhaps even his visit to Disney World, he will understand what he reads. He may even react to the sentence by, "Disney World is one of my favorite places to visit."

Reading, then, requires that your child not only recognize the words, but also (a) associates the words with his oral language, (b) relates the thoughts to his background of experiences, and (c) reacts in some way. Reading is more than recognizing words. Therefore it is important for you not only to help your child pronounce words, but also help him to understand what he reads.

Just as there are many skills needed to recognize words, there are a number of skills involved in comprehension. Your child should be able to find the *main idea* of a selection. This is the ability to tell in as few words as possible what the paragraph or story concerns. Noting the main idea is important so he can briefly tell others what he is reading, get the gist of the story or paragraph, or prepare an outline.

Another aspect of comprehension is noticing the *significant details* in the sentences, paragraphs, or stories. Answers to the who, what, how, when, and where type questions tell the most important facts in a story.

79

When reading an adventure story, recipe, or directions for putting something together, skill in noting the significant details is very important.

You can also help your child comprehend by having him notice the *sequence of events* when reading. What happened first, second, third, and so forth? Or what should we do first, second, and third when reading materials which require us to follow directions? Being aware of the sequence is very important in reading history, adventure stories, science experiments, recipes, and "how to do it" articles.

Skill in *drawing conclusions* is another aspect of comprehension. Children must be able to see why certain things happen. Reading is a thinking process because the reader must look for cause and effect relationships. Drawing conclusions is particularly important in reading stories or books which give reasons or suggest influences for particular actions or feelings.

Evaluating critically is a higher level comprehension skill. Children should not believe everything they read. Rather, they should consider whether it is fiction or non-fiction, the authenticity of facts, the author's motives, and propaganda techniques. A critical reader is constantly evaluating as he reads. Even though this is a higher level comprehension skill because it requires more background information, children do begin to develop skills in critical thinking at the primary grade level, and these thinking skills can be applied to critical reading. Critical reading skills are emphasized at the fourth, fifth, and sixth grade levels.

The following selection can be used to illustrate the comprehension skills which were described above. Read the selection and notice the kinds of questions which can be asked to check comprehension:

One morning Jimmy woke up and smiled. "This is a special day," he said. It was his birthday. The first thing he wanted was to have pancakes for breakfast. He just loved pancakes!

After eating five pancakes, Jimmy went to the zoo. His mother and father went too. They saw tigers, lions, and monkeys. His dad bought some peanuts. They fed them to the monkeys. It was fun at the zoo!

Then Jimmy went to the store with his parents. They told him he could pick out a toy. He decided to get a big truck. This was his birthday present.

Jimmy had fun playing with his truck. He drove it all around the house. Then it was time for supper. Jimmy's mother made a big birthday cake for dessert. Everyone sang "Happy Birthday."

After supper Jimmy went miniature golfing. It was fun to hit the golf balls into the holes.

All in all, it was a big day! Jimmy was tired when he went to bed.

Questions:
1. What is a good title for this story? (Main Idea)
2. What did Jimmy do on his birthday? (Details)
3. Where did Jimmy go after breakfast? (Sequence of Events)
4. Why was Jimmy tired? (Drawing Conclusions)
5. Do you think the story is true? (Evaluating Critically)

The comprehension skills are not as easily categorized according to grade level as the word recognition skills. Rather, these skills are emphasized at each grade level. Children should be able to recognize significant details at the first grade level and at the sixth grade level with increasingly difficult reading materials. The suggested activities and games in this chapter can be used with children at many different grade levels, but the difficulty of the reading materials must be adjusted to the child. Again the "a", "b", and "c" are used to indicate the most appropriate grade level at which the skills are introduced; but you must remember that the appropriateness of the activity depends upon the reading level of the materials you are using.

General Guidelines to Help Your Child
Improve His Comprehension

You must make sure your child has stories and books at appropriate reading levels in order to help him develop the comprehension skills. Notice that I used the word "reading levels" because your child actually has three different reading levels: independent, instructional, and frustrational. You need to be aware of these levels to help select books which your child is capable of understanding.

Your child's independent reading level is the grade level materials he can read all by himself. At the independent level your child should be able to recognize 99 percent of all the words and comprehend at least 90 percent of the material. All the reading materials which you expect him to read by himself such as homework assignments and "free" reading books should be at his independent reading level.

His instructional reading level is the grade level of materials he can read with little help from others. When your child is reading materials at his instructional level he is able to recognize 95 of 100 words and comprehend at least 75 percent of the selection. He will be able to read materials at this grade level if you tell him some of the words and help him establish a purpose for reading. You will be using books on his instructional level when you are helping him with new words or ideas.

Your child also has a frustrational reading level. This is the grade level of materials that are too difficult for him. Word recognition is less than 90 percent and comprehension is less than 75 percent. You will want to avoid giving your child reading materials at his frustrational level.

In addition to having three reading levels, your child also has a listening comprehension level. This is the grade level of material your child can listen to and understand when *you* read. Comprehension should be at least 75 percent. Keep this level in mind as you select books to read to your child.

Ask your child's teacher to tell you his reading levels. For example, the teacher may say the independent level is first grade, the instructional level is second grade, the frustrational level is third grade, and the listening level is fourth grade. These levels give you some estimate of the materials you can use with your child.

If your child is not in school, or if the teacher has not had an opportunity to determine his reading levels, you can use another technique to find appropriate reading material. A simple technique is to try to have him read a sample paragraph in a book. If he misses more than two out of 20 consecutive words, the book is too difficult for him. The book is also inappropriate if he cannot answer three of the four questions which you asked about the facts or vocabulary in the story. Regardless of the technique you use to find appropriate reading material, make sure the books are interesting to your child. Let him have the say so about the books you buy or borrow. Only when there is interest, is it possible to help your child comprehend.

Most children need to have a quiet place to read and study. Specific suggestions for providing a place for your child to read and study are included in Chapter Eight concerning the study skills. It will be necessary to help your child realize the importance of getting away from distractions when he is reading and studying. Remember there are some children who can do so while listening to music. Check your child's comprehension at different times to determine the conditions which facilitate his comprehension. Talk to him about these so he can plan for them.

This chapter includes suggested ideas, activities, and games which you can use to help your child develop the comprehension skills: main ideas, significant details, sequence of events, drawing conclusions, and evaluating critically. In addition to the ideas in this chapter, you will be able to use some of the ideas in Chapter Six concerning vocabulary. Vocabulary accounts for approximately 60 percent of comprehension. In other words, if your child does not understand the vocabulary words, he will not comprehend or get meaning from what he is reading. If your child is having difficulty comprehending, make sure you use some of the ideas in Chapter Six to improve his vocabulary.

The oral and silent reading skills can also influence his comprehension. Chapter Seven in this book has many ideas for helping you aid your child in developing the oral and silent reading skills which may in turn help him comprehend what he reads. For example, there are suggestions for helping your child determine and use an appropriate rate of reading. Since rate of reading influences comprehension, the ideas in Chapter Seven would also be of some value as you help your child comprehend what he reads.

Finally, it may be necessary to review some of the suggestions for helping your child recognize words which were presented in Chapters Three and Four. Of course, it is impossible to comprehend if the words are not recognized. You can begin to see how the reading skills are interrelated even though, for emphasis, they are being treated separately in this book. There simply is not a magic formula to aid your child in comprehending what he reads, but you can help if you follow several of the suggestions in the different chapters.

Main Ideas

185a. *Before School.* You can help your child develop skill in identifying main ideas prior to formal reading instruction. Talk with him about the main idea of a picture, a television program, or a story you are reading. Ask him to tell you a good name for the program, story, or picture in as few words as possible.

186abc. *What Is a Good Title?* Determining titles for stories your child has written makes him notice the main idea. After you have written a story with your child, ask him to think of a good title. Teach him not to write a title before he writes a story because he is not sure of what the story will be. You can vary this activity by asking your child why certain stories you read have particular titles.

187ab. *Making Scrapbooks.* If your child likes to make scrapbooks about pets, transportation, or insects, have him make a title page for his scrapbook. In labeling the scrapbooks, he is indicating the main idea.

188ab. *Matching Pictures and Paragraphs.* Cut out pictures and paragraphs which describe the pictures from an old torn book or from your child's magazines. Ask your child to read the paragraphs and then match them with the pictures. Of course your child must be able to comprehend what he reads in order to match the appropriate paragraphs and pictures.

189abc. *What Was Your Favorite Part?* After reading a story to your child, or after he reads a story to you, ask him what his favorite part was. Listen carefully to see what he says, as this will give you an indication of whether or not he can determine the main idea or whether he tells you every fact without saying something about the central thought. As you listen to his description of the favorite part, keep this information in mind as it will help you select other appropriate materials for your child.

190abc. *What's This About?* If you enter the room while your child is watching a television program or reading a book, ask him what it is about. Your child will probably want to respond quickly. Thus, you will be providing an opportunity for him to identify the main idea. He will see the need to tell you about the story or paragraph in as few words as possible. This is the same need you have when you prepare a telegram.

*191bc. *Finding the Most Important Sentence.* Ask your child to find the most important sentence in a paragraph. If he is not able to do so, have him notice that the topic sentence is usually the first or last sentence in a paragraph. Topic sentences or main ideas can be represented graphically with a triangle. If the main idea is the first sentence followed by supporting details, it can be represented by ▽. The main idea is the base line and then the supporting facts follow. If the main idea is the last sentence it may be represented by △ because the main point is last. Have your child find both types of paragraphs in a selection or book. If your child is required to write paragraphs, remind him to use a topic sentence to indicate the central thought of the paragraph.

192bc. *Mini Movies.* Your child might enjoy making a mini movie or a mural to show the main events of his favorite story. He will not want to do this for every story, but it can be a good rainy day activity. Shelf paper can be attached to two dowel rods or sticks. A movie screen can be made by cutting out the front of a cardboard box. Put the dowel rods through the top and bottom of the box and attach the shelf paper. As the dowel rods are turned, the movie rolls by.

*193abc. *Survey First!* You can help your child develop the habit of surveying materials before he reads them. This can be done with first grade books as well as sixth grade books. When surveying materials, have your child notice the pictures, major headings, and perhaps even read the summary if one is available. By surveying, your child is developing a frame of reference for what he will be reading. Of course this also helps him develop purposes for reading and thus aids concentration.

194bc. *Diagraming.* The main idea can be easily diagramed by making a large vertical box and writing the central thought in it. The supporting details can be written in smaller boxes under the central idea. You can also use the shape of a tree to diagram a paragraph. The trunk can be used to write the main idea with supporting details on each branch. See opposite page.

195bc. *Skimming.* Encourage your child to skim or read rapidly to find the main idea of a paragraph or story. Simply ask him to find the paragraph that tells about such and such. Use a timer to see how long it takes. You can also help your child use this skill when selecting books. Teach him how to look over books quickly to see if he is interested in them. Again he will be noting the main idea.

Significant Details

196ab. *Hunting.* Ask your child a particular question about a story and have him "go hunting" to find the answer. Give him a chance to ask you questions also because he must be comprehending in order to make up questions.

197bc. *Experiments and Tricks.* A book with science experiments is very valuable for helping your child notice details. All children enjoy books with tricks. Keep these two topics in mind as you buy books or check books out of the library. Noting significant details will be important if you use material that is meaningful to your child.

198bc. *TV Guide.* Use a TV Guide from a Sunday newspaper to help your child identify significant facts. For example, you could ask:

a. What show is offered on Channel 7 at 4 o'clock on Wednesday afternoon?
b. What sports events are offered this Sunday?
c. Select three programs you would like to watch during the week.
d. What shows are featured at 7 o'clock each night?

199b. *Scavenger Hunt.* The popular scavenger hunt is an excellent activity to help children notice details and follow directions. Make a list of things to be found. For example, "Find a rock that is bigger than an egg, three blades of grass, and five different kinds of leaves." Set a time limit, such as ten minutes. In addition to having fun, your child will be learning to note significant details.

It is fun to have a dog.

| You can play with it. | A dog never gets angry with you. | You can make it happy when you feed it. |

200abc. *Building Sentences*. The idea of this activity is to build long sentences by beginning with small three word sentences. For example, you might begin by saying, "A dog barked." Others in your family can add a word to the sentence but they must say the words that were used previously. For example, the small three word sentence may become, "A big black ferocious dog barked loudly at the masked robber who was carrying a small pistol." Help your child realize that in making sentences longer, more details are being added. Similarly, when he is reading, he will note that long sentences include many details.

*201bc. *Questions*. The who, what, where, and how questions can be asked to see if your child is comprehending. Be sure to ask questions that really make a difference in whether or not your child comprehends a story. Avoid asking questions concerning insignificant facts which do not influence the comprehension of a story. For example, if the fact that the boy wore a red shirt in the story is significant, you might ask what the color of the boy's shirt was. Most times, however, this question is not significant, but rather is simply used to provide a more vivid description of characters in a story. Make sure that the questions you ask are the ones that actually facilitate comprehension. Avoid asking too many questions about every selection or your child will begin to dislike reading.

202bc. *Useless Information*. Ask your child to look for the most important facts in a story. Also, see if he can pick out the useless facts that are often found in stories or math problems. For example, in the following selection have your child identify the most important facts, and those facts that are interesting, but not important.

> Jack went to the store. It took him ten minutes to find what he wanted. He bought four pieces of candy for 2¢ each. He gave the lady a dime. How much did he get back?

*203bc. *Following Directions*. The next time you put a toy or model together according to particular directions, have your child assist you. Ask him to read some of the directions to you or point to the picture that illustrates the direction you are reading. When your child gets a new game, give him an opportunity to figure out the directions independently. These activities not only help your child find important details, but emphasize that reading can be very useful.

204abc. *Art Can Be Fun*. If your child likes to experiment with different art media, you can have him illustrate some of the stories or parts of stories that he is reading. By examining the illustrations, you can note what your child is comprehending. For example, some children like to make dioramas depicting their favorite scene in the story, mobiles indicating the most important events in the story, or pictures of their favorite parts. Your child will be interested in doing these art activities only if the story has been particularly interesting to him.

205bc. *Describe Me*. Tell your child a noun and have him give as many adjectives as he can to describe the noun. For example, you might ask your child to name as many words as he can to describe table. He might indicate how many, which one, what kind, and so forth. This activity will help your child become more aware of descriptive words in stories that he reads. Since the descriptive words are details, you will be helping your child become more aware of details in his reading.

206bc. *Dialogue.* Some stories can be read as dialogues and this may facilitate your child's comprehension. It will be necessary to determine who is saying what and how they might say it. Of course this requires comprehension. You may want to tape your dialogue for other family members to hear.

207b. *Show Me Your Favorite Part.* Role playing is a very effective way of checking comprehension. Ask your child to act out his favorite character or favorite part of the story while you try to guess what it is. If you want to make the dramatization more complete, your child can make hand puppets or paper bag puppets of different characters in the stories he is reading. Keep in mind you are the expert on your child. You know the kinds of activities which will be of interest to him and those which will not work at all.

208bc. *Cooking.* Children love to cook and this activity requires noting significant details and following directions. Your child might enjoy making peanut butter pudding, but he must read this recipe in order to do so:

Beat ¼ cup of smooth peanut butter into 2 cups of cold milk. When the peanut butter and milk are mixed well, beat in one package of vanilla instant pudding. Pour into dixie cups and cool.

209b. *Finding the Facts.* One way to motivate your child to find facts in reading his textbooks is to give him a small treat for each fact he finds. For example, ask him to read his social studies or health book and give him an M & M for each fact he notices. You will be surprised at how much more your child will comprehend when he is motivated. If your child does have difficulty, you can guide him by asking questions concerning the who, what, where, when, why, and how of the story.

*210abc. *Let's Make Something.* The book, *838 Ways to Amuse a Child* by June Johnson, includes many things that you can make with a child. In doing so, he will need to notice the significant details and follow certain directions. This is another way that makes reading seem worthwhile and, in particular, noticing details a very important task. Other books that you may want to use are *What to Do When There's Nothing to Do* by Elizabeth Gregg and members of the staff of the Boston Children's Medical Center, and *1001 Ways to Have Fun with Children* by Jeanne Scargall. See Appendix I for complete references.

211bc. *Mnemonic Devices.* If there are certain facts your child must remember, you may want to help him form a mnemonic device to aid memory. For example, sometimes children are taught to remember the lines of a music staff by remembering the sentence "*every good boy does fine.*" Children remember the spaces on the staff by remembering the acronym, "face." If your child is required to memorize certain facts, perhaps you can teach him how to make up a mnemonic device.

212abc. *Games.* You can play many different games if you make sets of cards with questions and another set with answers. Games such as baseball, golf, and racetrack which were mentioned previously can be adapted to check comprehension. For example, ask a who, what, where, why, or how question to see if your child can move around the room in playing a baseball game. Allow him to move one base for every correct answer. Incorrect answers indicate an out. In addition to reading the games in this book, by this time you should be able to make up many of your own games that you know your child will particularly enjoy. Simply think of some activity your child likes and then have some particular objective in mind.

Sequence of Events

213ab. *Sentence Strips.* Write or type some sentences from a story your child has written or read. Cut the sentences into strips and mix them. Ask your child to put them in sequential order. For example:

On Saturday we went to the beach.
We played in the sand first.
Then it got so hot that we went swimming.
Daddy cooked hot dogs for supper.
It was a fun day.

214abc. *Comic Strips.* Cut apart comic strips which demonstrate a particular sequence of events. Mix them and ask your child to put them in order according to the way the story happened.

215b. *Time Booklet.* You can help your child make a booklet to show what he usually does during particular times of the day. Make a clock face on each page and indicate a particular time. At the bottom of the page write the activity that usually takes place. For example, you might include the time when he gets up, goes to school, eats lunch, comes home from school, watches a certain television program, has dinner, or goes to bed. Help your child realize that the events in our daily lives usually have some type of sequence. For example, he must get up before he can eat breakfast. Tell him that in many stories and selections he will find events, and he should notice the order in which they happen.

216ab. *Find the Order.* Read to your child or listen to him read, using some stories which have a particular sequence of events. An example is *The Old Lady and the Pig.* Ask your child what happened first, second, third, and so forth.

217bc. *Find the Time.* Give your child a newspaper, one of his magazines, or an old book and ask him to circle all the words he can find that indicate time; words such as then, first, finally, next, now, and last. By noticing these key words your child will be finding clues for the sequence of events. As you read to your child, you may emphasize these words by saying them a little louder.

218c. *Time Line.* Upper grade children generally enjoy making time lines. This activity is especially valuable when reading social studies or history books. Simply indicate the dates on a line in chronological order and write the events below them.

Drawing Conclusions

219ab. *Odd Ball!* As you are riding in the car, say a list of words that are related, along with one that does not belong. For example, apple, orange, tree, and banana. Ask your child which one is the "odd ball" and why it does not belong with the others. This activity will help your child categorize things which in turn can help him draw conclusions.

*220abc. *Because Sentences.* Say a sentence using the word "because" but do not finish it. For example, you might say, "It is going to rain because" and then have your child indicate a possible reason. In doing so, your child must draw a conclusion. Other possible beginning sentences are:

I feel badly because ——————— I am hungry because ———————
I am going to the store because ——————— I am tired because ———————
I am not going swimming because ——————— You go to school because ———————

Keep in mind that comprehension is thinking and by using activities such as this one you are helping your child develop his thinking abilities.

*221abc. *Feelings.* As you read to your child, or as your child reads to you, ask him how the different characters feel. Have him tell you why he has drawn this conclusion by pointing to significant facts or events in the story. If your conclusions differ, reread appropriate parts of the story to explain how you arrived at your conclusions.

222bc. *Missing Numbers.* Give your child a series of numbers and ask him which one is missing. Make sure the numbers follow some logical order so your child can draw a conclusion about the missing numbers. For example, you might say, "two, four, eight, ten, twelve," or "one, three, five, nine, eleven," and ask your child for the missing numbers.

223abc. *I'm Thinking of Something.* Begin this activity by describing some characteristic of a person, place, or thing. After doing so, see if your child can tell you what you have described. For example, you might say, "I am tall, I have wires, and men climb me. What am I?" To respond your child must put the clues together and draw a conclusion.

224ab. *Scrambled Sentences.* Use some of the flash cards from the word recognition games to form a sentence. Then mix the words and ask your child to put them in the right order. To do so he must comprehend the sentence. For example, you might have these words displayed in front of your child — "Sunday today is." He should put them in the correct order.

*225abc. *Tell Me Why.* One of the most important things you can do to help your child draw conclusions is to talk to him about things that he sees. For example, as you are taking a walk or riding in the car, you might ask him why cars have tires, why trees need rain, or why we have expressways. The more concepts the child brings to the reading situation, the more he gains from it. Remember that you are still helping your child learn to read by using many of these activities that do not even deal with written words, but rather with thinking skills. Reading is a thinking process.

226bc. *Why Words.* Give your child an old magazine or newspaper and ask him to circle words that give clues to the reasons for particular events. Words such as "because," "since," and "so," are possibilities. Talk with him about conclusions that are presented. Also ask him to make up sentences with "why words."

227bc. *Fables.* Most children love to hear fables because they are brief, but full of adventures. All fables require the reader to draw a conclusion. Read some fables to your child and ask him what the conclusion or moral is.

228bc. *Analogies.* Making analogies is another good activity to help your child think. For example, you might say, "The sun is to day as the moon is to —————." Have your child finish the analogy and tell you why he used a particular word. Some other possibilities are:

a. Pencil is to paper as hammer is to —————.
b. Sound is to radio as water is to —————.
c. Scissors are to paper as a knife is to —————.
d. Women are to men as girls are to —————.
e. Reading is to books as watching is to —————.

*229abc. *Stop and Think.* As you are reading to your child, or as you are listening to him read to you, occasionally stop and ask what he thinks is going to happen next. In order to do so, your child will have to draw some conclusions by making an inference. In addition to providing an opportunity to draw conclusions, this activity will also help your child establish a purpose for reading. He will want to see if his prediction is true. This technique of stopping after reading a few pages can also be valuable in helping your child concentrate as he is reading. Some children have a difficult time reading an entire selection of seven or eight pages, but can read the material if they read two or three pages at a time and then talk about it. Perhaps you will find it valuable to guide your child's reading taking this approach.

Evaluating Critically

230ab. *Fact or Fiction.* As you are reading or as your child is reading, ask if he thinks the events in the story really happened. This will help him separate fact from fiction. Discuss at this time why certain things are possible while other things are impossible.

90

231abc. *Tall Tales.* Have your child make up a tall tale or read one of the Paul Bunyan stories. Have him indicate which facts are true and which facts are exaggerated. In doing so, you will have many opportunities to clarify concepts.

232bc. *Fact or Opinion.* Say some statements and ask your child to tell you whether they are fact or opinion. For example, you might say, "Saturday is the best day of the week." Help your child realize this is an opinion because Saturday may not be the best day of the week for everyone. When reading, your child must determine which statements are fact and which are simply the opinions of the author.

*233bc. *Propaganda.* Elementary school children are able to recognize some propaganda techniques. Have your child notice the "band wagon technique," which is used in so many advertisements for children. The "plain folks appeal" which emphasizes admiration for the humble man in America is also used to influence children. Similarly, the appeal to identify with famous characters such as football players or movie stars is used to influence children. If you can help your child realize how others try to influence him to believe or act in certain ways, you will be helping him in evaluating critically. Point out the fine print on cereal box offers and other offers which make some deals less than attractive.

234c. *Emotional Appeal.* When looking at the newspaper with your child, read some of the headlines which sound sensational. Talk with your child about how writers try to get the attention of readers and help him see how some writers attempt to arouse emotions. You will find many good examples in children's magazines too. Talk about the advantages and disadvantages of emotional appeals.

235c. *Many Connotations.* Upper elementary school children are capable of realizing that words can have many different connotations. Simply say some words such as school, slaves, communism, odor, hero, and policeman and have your child tell you the thoughts he has associated with the words. Ask him to find words in his stories that have certain connotations. Help him realize there are different ways of saying things, depending on what the author is trying to express. For example, a sentence could read, "Joan is the *slender* girl standing near the water fountain," or "Joan is the *skinny* girl standing by the water fountain."

236c. *Pros and Cons.* Read an article describing the pros and cons of a particular issue that is of interest to your child. Help your child notice whether the argument is balanced. Are there more pros than cons? Also, look for over-generalizations and other propaganda techniques. Encourage your child to think of what the author did not include.

237c. *I Can't Believe It!* As you read the newspaper or other materials, point out to your child that you do not believe everything you read. Many times children are impressed by printed materials. They believe that everything that is written is true. Help your child realize that you do not believe everything you read. In doing so, you will be setting a model for your child so he will evaluate selections critically.

*238bc. *This Is How I See It*. Many times your child will not get the same answers to questions as you get. Chances are your answers are better. You can help your child understand how you arrived at your answers by rereading parts and pointing out how you interpreted it. Be ready to explain the criteria that you used in evaluating different statements. Also, point out inferences that you made based on your background of experiences. In doing so, you will be providing a model for your child.

CHAPTER SIX

HELPING YOUR CHILD INCREASE HIS VOCABULARY

The importance of the parents' role in helping their child develop an excellent vocabulary cannot be overemphasized. Research indicates the best way of learning new words is by having direct experiences. Since parents are the key figures in providing and/or arranging experiences for their child, parents are one of the most important factors in vocabulary development of children. This is especially true during the preschool and elementary school years.

Since providing many direct experiences is essential to help your child develop an excellent vocabulary, a list of some sample experiences follows. As you read this list, think of the vocabulary words your child might develop by having the experiences. You may want to put a check mark by those experiences which are appropriate for your child at this time. Refer to the list again to get other ideas of things to do or places to go. You will notice that most of the experiences are based on the assumption, "the best things in life are free." However, some of the experiences do require spending money.

Also notice the title of the list. This title is appropriate because your child's vocabulary will increase naturally if you are talking and pointing out things to each other. At the same time, remember it is necessary to provide for opportunities for your child to use the new words he is learning. Remember, if the word is expected to be a part of your child's reading and writing vocabulary, he must see the written form of the words. Also, take advantage of opportunities to use the words again so the child begins to develop them as a part of his listening and speaking vocabularies.

Having Fun While Your Child's Vocabulary Increases

—Help your child care for pets. You may want to visit the pet store to-gether, or purchase a book concerning the pets that you have.
—Take trips to parks, zoos, and various kinds of farms.
—Plant and care for a small garden.
—Plan a birthday party together.
—Visit a home under construction.

To help increase your child's vocabulary, encourage him to participate in activities at your local library.

—Take walks to notice evidence of the seasons, new trees, different features on homes, and so forth.

—Go to the library and then read stories to your child about animals, boats, airplanes, and other interests that he may have.

—Visit the post office, fire station, or other government places.

—Take a trip around the city to notice the different kinds of buildings, apartments, houses, hotels, office buildings, department stores, factories, railroad stations, and so forth. Point out different places as you go on various errands, or go for rides.

—Take your child to the bank with you so he can learn about its services.

—Visit an art museum, a planetarium, or a greenhouse.

—Make and help stock an ant house.

—Make visits to points of interest in various parts of your city, state, or country. Children do enjoy travel and learn so much by having different types of experiences.

—Watch television programs concerning other lands, animals, or people.

—Visit antique shops to show the child the way different things were made and what was available in the past.

—Play phonograph records of folk music, nursery rhymes, rhythms, and songs.

—Visit an Indian reservation.

—Visit a ham radio operator to learn something about world-wide communication.

—Plan, build, and stock an aquarium.

—Visit a weather station to learn what instruments are used and how they work.

—Go out to the airport and watch the planes come in, or go into the airport lobby and notice the different people and shops.

—Visit a meeting of the city or county legislative body and note the dispositions of requests of special interest groups. A school board meeting might be particularly appropriate for an elementary school age child.

—Encourage your child to develop a hobby or special skill such as photography, folk dancing, collecting stamps, instrumental music, or art.

—Participate in church groups, little leagues, scouts, or special lessons.

—Go to a sports event such as a baseball game, football, track, tennis, or swimming match.

—Play games together. Use both table and outdoor games such as badminton, baseball, and croquet.

—Cook unusual foods.

—Go on a camping or fishing trip. Take hikes together to explore nature.

—Go for a bicycle ride or take a walk around the neighborhood.

—Have picnics and/or go to the beach.

—Visit a boat dock.

—Take a Sunday afternoon ride in the country and notice the different types of animals and products.

—Pick tomatoes, strawberries, corn, peppers, or other products.

—Have house guests from different places.

—Attend some good movies together.

—Visit places where different products are made. The production of newspapers, pretzels, soda pop, baked goods, and candy are very interesting to children.

—Build something together: a treehouse, playhouse, doghouse, bookcase, doll bed, and so forth.

This list is of course endless. The point is, your child is like you — he learns by doing. The more experiences he has in life, the richer his life will be and as a result his vocabulary will be larger. Think of how rich a child's life would be if he were able to have most of the experiences which are mentioned above. Consider all of the vocabulary words he might learn by having these experiences. The schools can provide at most two field trips a year. Parents, on the other hand, can provide field experiences every day. Let us take advantage of them.

When explaining words to your child, try to relate the explanations to what the child already knows. This will help him classify different experiences. Notice the reactions of your child. He will let you know when you have said enough.

Let us take an example. If you use the word "appetite" during dinner by saying, "You certainly have a big appetite tonight," you might explain it by:

a. giving a synonym — "That's the same as saying you are hungry tonight."

b. using it in context again — "The hungry boy has a big appetite."

c. defining it — "An appetite is a feeling or desire for food."

d. demonstrating it — Roll your eyes and tongue when you see food.

Take advantage of opportunities to use the word again during the meal by saying, "Is your appetite being satisfied?" During the following days you can ask your child how his appetite is. It will not be long until your child is asking you how your appetite is!

If your child desires to see the written word, write it for him and point out the number of syllables and particular sounds. You can also call attention to prefixes or suffixes if they are a part of the word. In doing so you will be helping your child develop the word as a part of his reading and writing vocabularies.

To summarize, the most valuable way you can help your child develop an excellent vocabulary is to do things together and talk as you are doing. The experiences do not need to be out of the ordinary, but rather, take advantage of all the natural opportunities that arise as you are with your child. You need not plan for the introduction of special words, but you should be conscious of opportunities for the child to hear and use the word again. Keep in mind children need several repetitions with a word before they understand it, and that words have multiple meanings at many different levels of understanding. A parent is a teacher — the child's most important teacher. Have fun and enjoy the most ideal teaching situation: a one-to-one relationship filled with love and a big wonderful world to explore and enjoy.

Vocabulary Development

*239abc. *Avoiding Accidents*. Accidents are the number one cause of death of children. You can help your child avoid accidents by teaching some of the words commonly found around the house which warn children of danger. This does not guarantee that accidents will not happen, but it may help prevent accidents. Take advantage of opportunities to point these words out to your child again and again.

handle with care	do not inhale fumes
poison	do not use near heat
do not use near open flame	gasoline
keep medicines out of the reach of children	kerosene
external use only	this end up
acid	use in open air
chlorine	fragile
warning	combustible

*240abc. *Buildings*. Children and adults are required to read many signs when in public and private buildings. Again take advantage of opportunities to point the following words out to your child so he can learn to read them as soon as possible. These words can save embarrassment and perhaps a life.

no dogs allowed	fire extinguisher
combustible	handle with care
do not touch	information
employees only	keep closed at all times
exit	fire escape
elevator	first aid
out of order	gentlemen
	men
ladies	women
do not enter	in
out	emergency exit only
fragile	no minors
hands off	no touching
do not push	office
open	closed
entrance	private
pull	push
fallout shelter	use other door
watch your step	this end up
wet paint	step down (up)

*241abc. *Be Careful*. There are some words your child will encounter as he moves about your neighborhood and community that he should know for safety's sake. As you go for walks with your child, or take bicycle rides, take advantage of the opportunities to point out the following words. Talk about them, and help your child learn to read them as soon as possible.

beware	condemned
deep water	quiet
no swimming	no trespassing
explosives	beware of dog
flammable	contaminated
high voltage	inflammable
pedestrians prohibited	keep off
keep out	no diving
no fires	no fishing
no hunting	keep away
out of order	police
private drive	fallout shelter
shallow water	thin ice
walk	4-way stop
don't walk	danger
keep to the left (right)	no left (right) turn
warning	yield
merging traffic	stop

*242abc. *Textbook Clues*. Children at all grade levels from kindergarten to sixth grade meet new words in studying mathematics, social studies, health, science, and the other language arts. Skim your child's textbooks to get an idea of what words he is learning. Often new words are listed at the end of the chapter, or written in italics when they appear in context. As opportunities arise, you can use the words to help your child understand them.

*243abc. *Basal Readers*. Another source of important words can be found in his basal reader, if he is using one. You will find the new vocabulary words listed at the end of the book. Have your child read the words and check his understanding of them. Remember, he may recognize some of the words in context or in a story, but will not be able to recognize them on their own. Be sure not to ask him to read too many words at one time. You know your child's attention span.

You will notice that some of the new words are proper nouns, such as the names of characters or places. These more unusual names are not as important, so do not dwell on them. Also, do not have your child memorize the list of words. Instead, use words in games and activities and other situations which occur daily.

244ab. *Do This*. Print action verbs on index cards. For example, you might include the words clap, run, wave, shiver, frown, and throw. Have your child choose a card and indicate his understanding of the word by pantomiming the action.

245ab. *Getting Ready*. This activity will help your child get ready to do crossword puzzles. Give him a sentence and have him write the letters in the blanks to complete the words.

a. It is the opposite of up.   d---.
b. We keep it in the garage.   c--.
c. It is something we sit on.   ----r.

246bc. *How Many Words?* Write a special word such as a child's first or last name, the name of a season, or holiday, or the name of some famous person. Ask your child to write as many words as he can within a specified time period using only the letters that are contained in the given word. Point out other words he might have included so you can help him increase his vocabulary. A sample follows.

Easter

east   eat   star   steer   stare   ate   tea   tee   tear   ear
tree   see   rest   art   rate   ate   tars

*247abc. *Watching Television.* Even though some people complain about the evils of children watching television, there are some values to be derived. Children can learn many new words if you expand the meanings of words which they hear. Look over the television guide at the beginning of the week so you will not miss any of the children's specials. Also, some movies are great for building concepts and vocabulary.

*248abc. *Making a Bad Situation Good.* Children listen a little more carefully if you use some new vocabulary word when you are angry. They seem particularly interested because they want to know the consequences of their behavior and want to make sure they do hear what you say. For example, you might say, "I am appalled at your behavior!" Your child will get the message!

249a. *Toughies.* This activity will help your child understand some of the little words that may give a lot of trouble. You will need three objects of different colors and a small box. Red, blue, and yellow blocks may be used. Give the following oral directions to your child.

a. Take a red block *out* of the box.
b. Put the blue block *between* the red and the yellow one.
c. Put the red block *beside* the blue one.
d. Put them *on* the table.
e. Put the red block *over* the yellow one.
f. Put the red block *under* the blue one.
g. Take the blue block *off* the table.
h. Put three blocks *into* the box.

250bc. *Letter Addition.* Begin this activity by giving your child one letter. Ask him to add one letter at a time to build a new word. Every letter that he uses must be used again to make new words. You can add a new word and thus use this opportunity to teach your child a new vocabulary word. For an example:

a .... at .... ate .... date .... hated

251bc. *Word Architecture.* Write a long word on the middle of a piece of paper and ask your child to add new words by building words from the original word. A sample follows. This is an excellent activity when your child is confined to bed.

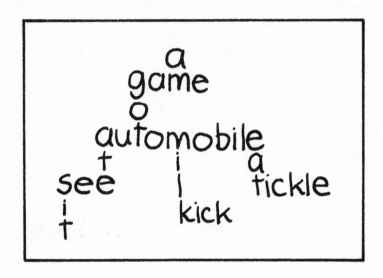

252abc. *Hangman.* Hangman is a favorite game of children and can be used for many different activities. To play, you will need to draw a gallows on a piece of paper. Flash a new vocabulary word that your child is learning and ask him to pronounce it and use it in a sentence. If the word is mispronounced or used incorrectly, draw the head or another part of the man's body in a noose on the gallows. Determine how many parts of the body you are going to use as this game can go on forever by adding ten toes, ten fingers, and so forth. Usually it is fun to play with five to seven parts of the body (head, neck, arms, torso, and legs). Try to see how many words your child can get correct before the man is hung. This game may sound gruesome, but children seem to love it. It is a very motivating method of reviewing words.

*253abc. *Do You Know What That Word Looks Like?* When your child hears new words that have unusual spelling, ask him if he wants to see what the word looks like when it is written. Some words such as pneumonia, gnaw, and wrought look very different from the way they sound. If you want to increase your child's reading and writing vocabularies as well as listening and speaking vocabularies, make sure your child sees the written form of new words.

254abc. *A Word a Day.* If you want to concentrate on vocabulary development you might have your child make a bulletin board on which he displays a new word for each day. A new word might be one which you used during the day or on the previous day. Include the definition of the word as well as a sentence using it in context. It may also be possible to draw an illustration of the word.

chisel (chiz'l) - a sharp-edged tool for cutting or shaping wood, stone, or metal.

I can use a chisel to make some things.

255bc. *Sensory Words.* Ask your child to list as many words as he can for each one of the five senses. For example, for touch he may say soft, hard, smooth, and scratchy. Other examples are:

> Vision — beautiful, ugly, clear
> Taste — bitter, sweet, sour
> Hear — bang, buzz, bubbling
> Smell — bread baking, awful, stinky

256bc. *Crossword Puzzles.* Children's editions of crossword puzzles are available at many department stores or newsstands. Many children's puzzle books also include jumbled words. This is a popular method of increasing vocabulary while having fun. Make sure your child can do most of them or he will become frustrated and avoid the puzzles. Keep in mind that when your child learns words by using the crossword puzzles, he usually only gets one simple definition of the new word. Provide other opportunities to expand the meanings of different words. Also, remember that you can rearrange the letters of some words your child is learning and then see if he can figure out what the words are. For example, you might write "graned" and your child will figure out that this is "danger." This activity does not cost as much as commercial crossword puzzles, yet is fun.

257abc. *Antonyms Around the House.* Tell your child the name of some word or action that he can see in the house and ask him to give you an antonym. For example, you might say: floor, open, push, light, under, clean, run, and angry and have him tell you the opposite for each word. This is a good activity to play when riding in the car, too. Use synonyms to add variety.

*258abc. *The 100 Word Club.* If your child is keeping a word file of the new words he is learning, ask him to tell you when he has 100 words he thinks he knows. Shuffle the cards and randomly select 10. Ask him to say the word, define it, and use it in a sentence. If he is able to do so, he becomes a member of The 100 Word Club. Cut out the certificate on page 189 and give it to him. If you want to make the certificate more attractive, glue it to a brightly colored piece of tag board or poster board. If your child is younger, you may want to have a Ten Word Club or Fifty Word Club.

259bc. *Homonym Hunt.* Make a deck of index cards with homonyms. Shuffle the cards and deal five to each player. Have the first player draw a card from the pile or from the other person's hand. If the player has a pair of homonyms, he can lay them down if he can give two sentences which illustrate the different meanings of the homonyms. If he cannot give two sentences, the homonyms are placed back in the deck and reshuffled. The first player to use all of his cards is the winner. Some possible homonyms are:

sun - son	so - sew	beat - beet
read - red	by - buy	knight - night
their - there	wrap - rap	bare - bear
your - you're	maid - made	capitol - capital
no - know	tee - tea	for - four
knew - new	meat - meet	hymn - him
mail - male	herd - heard	peace - piece
knot - not	hare - hair	sense - cents
grate - great	die - dye	fair - fare
tide - tied	steak - stake	hole - whole
wrote - rote	waist - waste	aunt - ant

260bc. *Homonym Basketball.* The same cards you made for the "Homonym Hunt" (above) can be used for this activity. Ask your child to put the words in pairs and give a sentence in which both words are used. For example: "The herd heard the hunters coming," "I will write right now," "They drank tea on the first tee," or "The hare did not have any hair." If he can use both homonyms in the same sentence he scores a field goal and gets 2 points. If he can only use one of the words correctly in a sentence he gets a foul shot and scores only 1 point. No points are earned if the words are used incorrectly. Keep a record of his score to see how much he improves. You can help him improve by giving possible sentences and discussing the meanings of the different homonyms.

*261abc. *Idioms Are Fun.* No doubt you have used idioms in daily conversations and your child asked you what you meant. Or, you had a good laugh when your child interpreted the idiom literally. You can help your child learn the meanings of different idioms by pointing out their meanings when you use them. Some of the common idioms are listed below. Make a point of using these with your child to make his language richer.

a. to make a mountain out of a molehill — to treat a trifle with importance
b. to stir up a hornet's nest — to cause serious trouble
c. to stick to one's guns — to maintain that one is right
d. with tongue in cheek — insincerely
e. to put the cart before the horse — to reverse logical order
f. to draw in one's horns — to reduce demands or expectations
g. out of hand — beyond control
h. to put on a good face — to make the best of a situation
i. to look a gift horse in the mouth — to criticize a gift
j. a horse of a different color — an entirely different kind of person or situation
k. to make a scene — to create a disturbance
l. to go scot free — to escape without punishment
m. to put one's hands on — to find
n. know the ropes — be familiar with some situation or place
o. kept in the dark — not aware of the facts
p. down in the dumps — depressed
q. red tape — excessive concern with petty details
r. by hook or by crook — to accomplish by any means
s. to rest on one's laurels — to be so satisfied with success that one no longer tries hard
t. to take down a peg or two — to lower the pride of
u. in the limelight — to be the center of attention

*262c. *Thesaurus.* Older children can use a thesaurus to find synonyms and antonyms for words. When introducing the thesaurus, have your child look through it to find out what it contains. Suggest that he look for a particular word that he knows. Then give a specific word and ask him to find as many synonyms and antonyms as he can without looking at the thesaurus. He can then check his response with his thesaurus. Discuss when a thesaurus would be useful.

263abc. *Commercial Vocabulary Games.* Many of the commercial vocabulary games that are available are good for vocabulary building. *Perquacky* is good since the child has to make words with letter cubes. Your child will soon learn to look for sound patterns as he tries to make three, four, five, and six letter words. The game of *Probe* requires one player to guess the other player's words by asking if he has certain letters. Again sound patterns and common letters are emphasized so an educated guess can be made. *Scrabble* and *Spill and Spell* are excellent for this too. *Password* is valuable because children must think of synonyms to give clues.

As you use these commercial vocabulary games with your child, try to use some words that are new to him. In doing so, define the words and use them in a sentence. Keep in mind that your child is going to need many repetitions with the word before he is able to understand it. Also realize that children understand words at different levels. You can help him learn other meanings of the word and also help him see how it relates to other words and ideas.

264c. *Etymologies.* If your child is older he may be interested in the origins of words or their etymologies. Etymologies help expand and clarify the meanings and spellings of some words. They also provide insight into how our language has developed. For example, the word *adopt* is derived from the Latin word *adoptare.* *"Ad"* means to and *"optare"* means choose. Thus, adopt means to choose.

Etymologies are found in some dictionaries, usually placed in square brackets before or after the definition. Check your dictionary to see if and where the etymologies are listed. Of course it is not necessary or possible to go into detail concerning the origin of every word. Only do so if your child seems interested.

CHAPTER SEVEN

HELPING YOUR CHILD IMPROVE HIS ORAL AND SILENT READING SKILLS

The What and Why of Oral Reading, Silent Reading, and Rates of Reading

Oral and silent reading skills are a concern at *every* grade level. Oral reading is usually emphasized during the primary grades (grades 1 to 3), while silent reading skills and rates of reading are more of a priority at the intermediate grade levels (grades 4 to 6). Oral and silent reading both require the child to "put everything together to get the job done." In doing so, he has opportunities to apply all the reading skills.

Oral Reading

Skill in oral reading is important to children because many adults use this as the single criterion to determine whether or not a child can read. Friends and relatives will ask a child to read and then sit quietly as if they were being entertained by a concert pianist. Little or no attention is paid to comprehension which is the essence of reading. Instead, in the eyes of many adults, the good reader is like a great orator.

Children realize the importance many adults attach to oral reading. In fact, many children feel they did not study reading in school if they did not have a turn to read orally that particular day. This concept of reading actually hinders a child because he believes reading is simply "sounding good." We must help children understand there is far more to reading than this. Communication with the author is the most important factor.

Oral reading is important at times. It is a child's way of actively showing others that he is learning to read. Also, children need to develop skill in reading orally so they can read stories, reports, and poems to others. Oral reading is necessary when reading to prove a point or to share information which others do not have. Finally, some children use oral reading as an aid to comprehension. Perhaps you yourself have understood something orally when at first you did not understand it when reading silently.

As your child reads orally, you will want him to use correct pronunciation, articulate clearly, read in meaningful phrases, adjust the speed to the selection, use proper intonation and expression, breathe properly, and assume an appropriate posture. Oral reading involves many complex skills rather than one simple skill of "oral reading." You can use the following list to evaluate your child's oral reading skills. As he reads, notice which skills he has developed and which ones need improvement:

a. Interprets feelings correctly (humor, excitement, suspense), and can use suitable pitch, tone, and volume to express the feelings.
b. Knows many sight words and uses word recognition techniques easily.
c. Reads in thought units or phrases without jerkiness or hesitation.
d. Observes punctuation marks.
e. Can be heard easily, enunciates clearly and distinctly, and has a pleasing voice.
f. Is free from strain or tension.
g. Reads at the proper rate of speed.
h. Does not omit words, substitute words, or repeat words.
i. Does not lisp or stutter.
j. Holds the book properly and has good posture.
k. Keeps his place without difficulty.

Be sure to work on only one or two skills at a time. If you try to make your child a perfect oral reader in one easy lesson the result will be a frustrated child and an angry parent. Select a few of the activities and games and use them in natural situations.

Providing time for your child to read to you is very important. Do not make him read every story or book orally, but rather ask him to read the most exciting parts. One major purpose of oral reading from the child's point of view is showing you that he can read. Learning to read is expected of children in our society. Just as your child says, "Hey Mom, watch this!" when he has learned something new, he wants you to listen as he reads.

Ask your child to read the selections *silently before reading them orally*. Only then can he know the feelings and expressions of the characters, the words, and at the rate at which he should be reading. If your child reads the selection orally first, he must figure out the expressions and words as he is going along. This is an unrealistic expectation because the child is conscious of wanting to sound good, but cannot because he does not know the moods of the characters. You would not want to read a selection to others unless you first had a chance to look it over (read it silently). Let us give our children this same opportunity.

When listening to your child read, do not continually correct him as he makes errors. Praise him for what he did well and then make suggestions when he has finished reading. If you do interrupt him constantly he will become frustrated and make more errors. The only time you should correct him when he is reading is when he mispronounces a word or skips a

Oral reading involves many complex skills, but try to make it fun for the child.

word which might hinder comprehension of the selection. In this case simply tell him the word and allow him to continue.

Remember to check to see if your child is comprehending as he reads. You can do this by asking questions or telling the child to read the part of the story that describes a certain event or reason for a particular action.

Silent Reading

Skill in reading silently is just as important as developing skill in reading orally. As an adult, most of the reading that you do is silent reading; therefore, you want your child to read well both silently and orally.

There are many silent reading habits and skills which need to be developed. Children must learn to move only their eyes, rather than their whole head. They must learn not to mouth every word as they read. As you watch your child read silently see if he is developing any of the following faulty habits:

a. Pointing at each word with his finger.
b. Moving his lips loudly.
c. Moving his head while moving from left to right on a page, or when going back to the beginning of the next line.
d. Expressing nervous tension.
e. Holding the book too close or too far away (14 inches is average).
f. Making too many fixations as he is reading. A fixation is a stopping of the eyes to focus on a particular word.
g. Making too many regressions while reading. A regression is looking back to the beginning of the sentence or to previously read words.

The same guidelines that were suggested for helping your child read orally are appropriate for helping him develop the silent reading skills and habits. Work on only one aspect of silent reading at a time, provide meaningful opportunities for silent reading, remember to check comprehension, and do not interrupt the child after you have asked him to read something silently.

Rate of Reading

Rate of reading is a concern at all grade levels. However, it is usually not emphasized until the third or fourth grade. Normally children's eyes are not mature enough for rapid reading until the age of eight or nine. Some of the other skills, such as word recognition skills, are more important when beginning reading instruction.

In recent years a good reader and a fast reader have become synonymous terms. Yet a mature reader is not necessarily a fast reader, but rather one who can adjust his rate of reading to the material. Your child should develop three different types of reading rates.

The *normal* rate is used when reading to find answers to specific questions, to note details, solve problems, and grasp the relationship of details to the main idea. The normal rate is also appropriate to appreciate the beauty of literature.

The *rapid* rate is used in skimming to find a particular response, get the main idea of a selection, or to review a familiar selection. For example, rapid reading is important when looking for a particular name in the telephone book or some specific information in a newspaper advertisement. Your child may also use the rapid rate of reading when he is skimming a selection in an encyclopedia to gather information.

After finding the information in the encyclopedia, your child will probably want to use the third rate of reading: the *careful* rate. The careful rate of reading is useful when trying to master content, evaluate materials, note significant details or sequences, or in following directions. The careful rate is also valuable for memorizing selections or when outlining materials.

Learning to read is like learning to drive a car. The driver does not learn to drive at expressway speed. He learns to adjust his speed in heavy traffic, local neighborhoods, or turnpikes. Skill in operating under different circumstances is required. A reader must learn to adjust his rate to different types of materials and to his purposes. A mature reader is flexible in his rate, not just fast.

To find your child's normal rate of reading, count the number of words he has read in a particular time limit. Divide the number of words by the number of minutes it took him to read the selection. This is the number of words he can read per minute. For example, if your child reads 400 words in 5 minutes, he has read 80 words per minute. Remember to ask your child questions to check his comprehension after you have timed him. A rapid rate of reading is worthless without comprehension.

When working on rate of reading you should use materials that the child can read easily. I would suggest using reading selections that are at his independent reading level. This makes it possible to concentrate on rate without being worried about word recognition or problems of comprehension.

One of the most important factors in rate of reading is that of reading in phrases rather than reading word by word. The rate of reading is improved because the child looks for more than one word at a time. You can realize the value of this by reading the following selection which has been divided into phrases:

These words	as a unit	His eyes
are arranged	rather than	can see
in columns	reading	several small words
of phrases	each word	at a time.
to help you	as a unit.	As he develops
realize the	This will	he will be able
importance of	help him	to read longer phrases.
reading phrases.	to read	Now it's time
Your child	more smoothly,	to have fun
should try	more rapidly,	with the
to read	and with	ideas and games
each line	better comprehension.	to help your child.

Oral Reading Skills

*265abc. *You Are the Model.* Continue to read to your child regardless of his age. As you read, you are setting the example. Do not hesitate to "ham it up" as you read the expressions of different characters. Sometimes you will want to read rapidly, and other times slowly. Your rate will depend on the characters and events of the story. Your child needs your model. Reading orally to him is one of the most important things you can do to help him develop skill in reading orally to others.

*266ab. *Traffic Signs.* You can teach the meanings of punctuation marks by comparing them to traffic signs. Commas can be likened to yield the right of way signs. Periods are like stop signs. Talk with your child about why we need punctuation marks or rewrite a selection without punctuation marks so he can realize their importance. Soon he will see that punctuation marks make understanding possible.

*267ab. *Find the Quotation Marks.* At the beginning stages of reading instruction ask your child to find the quotation marks. See if he can figure out that quotation marks tell us exactly what the person said. Discuss the importance of words such as "said Susan" which help us understand who is talking. This activity will help your child realize that reading is talk written down. Write one of your child's conversations with another person so he can see the value of quotation marks.

*268ab. *Kinds of Sentences.* Talk with your child about the different kinds of sentences and give him clues about how they are read. The voice is usually raised at the end of a sentence that asks a question. Exclamation marks indicate strong feelings. Sentences simply stating a fact are usually read in a normal tone. Command sentences can be read in a variety of ways depending upon the feelings of the characters. Have your child read the same sentence in different ways to show different feelings. For example, have your child read the following sentence in three different ways: I told you I did it.

Also have him try to read this sentence using three different ways: There's Aunt Millie.

269ab. *Choral Reading.* There are some poems or brief selections you can read with your child as a choral reading. Actually you can choose any selection that your child is able to read and read it as a choral reading. In doing a choral reading you and your child say the same words together, or each person can have a special line or a part.

*270abc. *What's on TV?* There are many times during the day when you can ask your child to read orally. You may ask him to read the description of a television program, the back of a cereal box, or even the directions as you bake a cake. Remember the home is not a miniature school; simply take advantage of the teachable moments as they occur.

271ab. *Stamp Out Monotones.* Read in monotone a conversation from one of your child's favorite stories such as *Little Red Riding Hood.* Ask your child whether the characters would really speak that way. Talk about the feelings of the characters and what facial expressions and gestures they might use to express their feelings. Then have your child read the conversation to show you how the characters would sound. Emphasize facial expressions as well as information while reading.

272ab. *Mark the Line.* If your child points to every word with his finger as he reads, give him a bookmarker to use. This could also be a 3 x 5 index card. By using the marker he will be more likely to read in

110

phrases because he is not pointing at each word, but simply moving the card along the line to mark his place. As soon as he is able to follow along without the marker, discard it.

273ab. *Articulation.* If your child continually pronounces some words incorrectly, it is probably because he cannot remember the sounds, has not developed the sounds, or he has heard others say the word incorrectly. Write the word in syllables and have him look at the parts and say them. Keep in mind that some sounds such as v, l, and z are not usually developed until the age of 6.

274ab. *Find the Sentence.* To make oral reading purposeful and also to check comprehension, ask your child to find the sentence that tells an answer to a specific question you ask. This will provide an opportunity for him to skim for key words, as well as giving him a chance to read orally to you.

275b. *Building Sentences.* State a simple sentence with a subject and a predicate that can be said in one phrase. Ask your child to add another phrase to expand the sentence. See how many phrases he can add to make a long sentence. Emphasize adding phrases rather than just words so your child begins to consider phrases when reading. For example, you may begin by saying, "The horse ate," and your child might add "the green grass/ before he went/ into the barn."

276bc. *Colorful Phrases.* If your child reads word by word, rewrite some of the sentences in phrases. Crayons can also be used on some of the magazine selections to color each phrase using a different color. Ask your child to read the phrase rather than one word at a time. You can also have him use slashes to mark some of the phrases in the articles in his magazines. These can then be used in reading to you.

*277abc. *Using the Tape Recorder.* Most children love to hear their own voices. Ask your child to read into the tape recorder so he can hear what he sounds like. When going over the tape, point out what he does well and help him see how he can improve. Ask him to do the evaluating, too. Self evaluation is usually more effective because he will know what should be improved. Have him reread the same selection after practicing. You may want to mail some of the tapes that he makes to relatives or friends if they are particularly interested in your child.

278bc. *Slow Down.* After your child does develop a more rapid rate of reading, he is likely to use this rapid rate when reading orally. Help your child understand that an excellent reader is not a rapid reader, but rather one who is able to adjust the rate to the nature of the selection. You can help your child understand that he should go slowly to express sadness or mystery. A rapid rate might be used to express excitement and hurry. A normal rate may be used for the narrative part of the story. Find examples of the different types of materials requiring different rates and demonstrate these to your child.

279bc. *Now It's Your Turn.* Children generally enjoy the activity of reading until they make an error that someone else in the family notices. The other person should correct the error and continue reading the material until he makes an error. You will have to make errors so your child gets his turn. Errors can include mispronounced words, omissions of words, and repeated words.

Silent Reading Skills and Habits

280a. *Guided Reading.* If your child cannot concentrate long enough to read an entire story, you can guide his silent reading by asking him to read one page at a time. When he is finished, ask questions to see if he is comprehending, and then give him a reason for reading the next page. Continue increasing the number of pages as he develops more skill in silent reading.

*281ab. *Find Out.* Before your child starts to read silently, look over the material with him and try to develop a reason for reading. For example, you may ask him to read to find out why the picture shows what it does, or to find answers to specific questions. Concentration will be improved if the child has a purpose for reading. Encourage your child to find his own reasons for reading by looking at the pictures and number of pages before beginning to read the first page.

*282ab. *Posture.* Posture is not emphasized today as it was in previous years. Children read while lying on their stomachs as well as with both feet on the floor. The important factors are distance from the eyes to the book, lighting, and whether or not the child is comfortable. Fourteen inches is the normal distance from the eyes to the book. Demonstrate this to your child as well as the way light affects the clarity of the printed page. Help him realize that glare makes it difficult to read.

283ab. *Hand on Head.* If your child moves his entire head rather than just his eyes when he is reading, ask him to hold his head with his hands while the book is in front of him. In this position it will be impossible to move the head so he will use his eyes only. Make sure the distance from the eyes to the book is appropriate.

284ab. *Fingers on Lips.* Ask your child to put his fingers over his lips if he vocalizes while reading silently. Fingers will make him aware of the lip movements and help him stop them.

285ab. *Follow the Eraser.* If your child omits lines or continually moves his head as he reads, hold a pencil before him about 20 inches from his face. Ask him to hold his head still and focus on the eraser as you move the pencil in an arc. Notice if his eyes move together and if the movements are smooth or jerky. Games with rolling objects such as kickball are good for developing eye movements. If your child continues to have difficulty focusing, read the detailed descriptions of visual problems and suggestions for help which are listed in Chapter Ten.

*286bc. *Review Time.* Children are likely to skip an unknown word when they are reading silently. Review the techniques of word recognition so your child can figure out words independently. You might begin by asking the child what he does when he comes to words he doesn't know. Review the fact that he can divide the word into syllables and sound it out, skip it, and read the rest of the sentence to figure out the meaning, analyze the structure of the word, or look the word up in the dictionary.

Rates of Reading

*287bc. *Good Advice.* Talk with your child about when to read rapidly, slowly, and at a normal rate. Only when children understand the use of different rates will they be skillful in adjusting their rates. Show different types of materials for which different rates are appropriate. Before your child reads different types of materials, ask him at what rate he plans to read the materials.

288bc. *Helpful Fingers.* In most cases we try to teach children not to use their fingers while reading, but when skimming it is very appropriate to "let the fingers do the walking." Direct your child to skim by moving his fingers down the middle of the page to find out the main idea or key words. He will be better at this if you retype the selection with lines of only three words, as was illustrated earlier in this chapter. As he becomes more skillful, you can increase the number of words per line.

289bc. *Controlled Reader.* Cut a small window out of the middle of a 4 x 6 index card. The window should be no longer than the space of 16 letters. Move it along as your child reads. You can control the speed and adjust to his rate. As his rate improves, move the card faster. Your child can also practice improving his rate by moving the card himself.

*290bc. *Can You Remember?* Practice reading at a careful rate when reading directions for a science experiment, a recipe, a new game, or in putting a model together. Ask your child to read specific directions and then check his comprehension. He will soon learn the importance of reading slowly. Talk with your child about the fact that sometimes it is necessary to reread some materials at a careful rate to note what was said. Rereading — even vocalizing the second time around — can be a valuable aid to comprehension and memorization. Help your child understand that sometimes the need to read it again is common.

291bc. *Find the Name.* Show your child how to move his hands down a page in a telephone directory to find a certain name. After he has practiced and is proficient in using his fingers, he will realize this is a time-saving device.

292c. *Key Words.* Ask your child to find the answer to a specific question as quickly as possible. For example, if you are working with the child's social studies textbook, ask him for particular facts from a certain page. Teach him to look for key words and dates.

293bc. *Time Find.* You will need to use some of the flash cards with words and phrases that you made for earlier games suggested in this book. Place the words and phrases on the table and ask your child to find a particular one as quickly as possible. When looking for phrases, he will realize the importance of looking for key words to increase his speed. The child will also realize that the more words he knows at the automatic response level, the more time he saves.

294c. *Newspapers.* Newspapers are made quickly and are intended to be read quickly; thus, they are excellent for practicing skimming. Ask your child to skim the first paragraph of a particular article. He will notice that the major points can be found in the first paragraph, while supporting details are described later. To read the newspaper rapidly, he should pay close attention to the first paragraph of the articles, and read or skim the remaining paragraphs for those facts that are of interest to him. Helping your child realize the way different materials are organized will also help him read at the appropriate rate.

295c. *Keeping Records.* Some children enjoy keeping records of their rates of reading. Time your child on selections which are conducive to rapid reading. Stories commonly found in children's magazines are appropriate. Set a particular time limit, such as five minutes, and then ask questions to check his rate of comprehension. A graph of the number of words and dates can be constructed. Keep the graph over a period of time so progress can be noted.

296c. *That's Not for Me!* Many parents ask about the value of a speed reading course for their children. Keep in mind that generally the elementary school child's eyes are not developed enough to profit from any course in speed reading. Also, speed reading is difficult for elementary school age youngsters because they must be very skillful in noting the major ideas, the organization of the material, and some of the other higher level thinking skills which have not been fully developed by the end of the elementary school years. Another reason speed reading should not be emphasized with elementary school children is that generally elementary school children are just beginning to develop a large enough reading vocabulary to appreciate the author's descriptions. If the material is read too rapidly, children miss this feature. Do not be too concerned about your child's rate at this time, but rather be concerned that he realizes that there are three different rates he can use, depending upon the nature of the material and his reason for reading.

CHAPTER EIGHT

HELPING YOUR CHILD DEVELOP STUDY SKILLS

One kind of reading all children do in school is functional reading. Functional reading is "reading to learn" or to gather information, and is especially important in the intermediate grades (Grades 4-6) because most study activities require reading. Many students do not do as well as they might in social studies, science, mathematics, or health, because they have difficulty reading content area materials. It is not only important for your child to learn to read, but equally important that he can "read to learn."

Understanding the Locational and Study Skills

You are in an advantageous position to help your child develop appropriate *study skills and habits.* This is not an easy task because many children avoid studying. The concern of the parent and apparent lack of concern of the child cause many clashes in the typical North American home.

Some children dislike studying because they do not know how to do it. The child who has to read pages 137-142 of his social studies book, frequently opens the book to page 137 and begins reading. By the time he is on page 138 he has little or no idea of what he is reading. He is looking at the words, but is not getting ideas or comprehending. He needs help.

One of the most important tasks of parents and teachers of elementary school age children is to help the child develop a *method of studying.* Many children study haphazardly throughout their school years. Many colleges and universities offer courses in how to study which teach the same study techniques elementary school children should learn.

There are five steps in effective study. First, your child should *survey or preview* the materials he is going to study. He can look at the pictures and major topics and read the summary to get an idea of what he is going to be learning.

The second step is to *develop questions* that he will be able to answer after reading the selection. The easiest way to develop questions is to turn the major headings into question form. For example, if the major heading is, "Products of Mexico," the child would say, "What are some products of Mexico?" Some textbooks have questions listed at the beginning or end of the chapter or selection. Encourage your child to read these *before* reading the text. Studying will become more effective if your child has specific questions to answer because he will be reading for a purpose.

The third step in studying is to *read to answer* the questions that have been formed. The child should be careful to adjust his rate to the nature of the material.

The fourth step is to *answer the questions or recite*. This recitation provides an opportunity for the child to make sure he is learning what he set out to learn. Younger children should recite or answer the questions immediately after reading a short selection, rather than trying to read the entire selection before reciting. This is essential because often knowledge from previous paragraphs is needed to understand subsequent paragraphs. Some children may want to take notes by writing out answers to their questions.

The final step is to *review* what has been read. This can be done by rereading the difficult sections or by rereading the notes. The child might also glance at the major headings and indicate some points listed under them. Encourage him to reread if he cannot answer all the questions.

Two formulas concisely summarize the five steps. One was developed by Francis Robinson* and is called SQ3R. "S" stands for survey, "Q" means question, and the "3R's" are read, recite, and review. Another popular formula suggested by Spache* is PQRST (preview, question, read, summarize, and test). These formulas may help your child remember the steps involved in effective study.

Another study skill that is necessary for effective study is the ability to *summarize and organize materials*. The child should be able to get the main idea and see the relationship between it and supporting details. This skill is especially important when writing reports, taking notes, or preparing for a test. Children should be taught how to outline as an aid to summarizing and organizing information. Here is a simple outline form your child can use:

    I. Indians (Topic)
       A. Food (Main Idea)
          1. Details
          2. Details
          3. Details

       B. Homes (Main Idea)
          1. Details
          2. Details
          3. Details

---

*Robinson, F. P., *Effective Study*. New York: Harper and Brothers.

*Spache, G and Spache E., *Reading in the Elementary School*. Boston: Allyn and Bacon, Inc., 1969.

If your child is preparing a written report, this outline can be used to help him say it in his own words rather than copying from the book. The topic sentence is clearly outlined, so writing paragraphs is easier.

Neatness and legibility are also a part of study activities when written reports are required. Explain to your child that most writers make a rough copy of their work, then they proofread it and make a final copy. Help him develop pride in his work by praising it when it is well done.

Another aspect of studying is that of *preparing for tests.* You can help your child by asking him questions about material. Do this in game form to make it more exciting. The following guidelines for taking tests can be explained to him. For true/false or multiple choice questions:

a. If a statement is *partly false,* mark it *false.*
b. *All, only, always,* and *never* mean "without any exceptions."
c. Watch for words like *usually, often, frequently* which may change the character of the answer required.
d. Eliminate choices that you know are wrong, and then choose from what are left.
e. Answer questions you are sure of first; go back to the doubtful ones.

For essay type questions:

a. Decide whether you are to tell *what, how, why, when, where, who;* and whether you are to describe, tell about, or compare.
b. Know the meaning of:

compare	illustrate
reasons	list
explain	evaluate
contrast	outline
define	

c. After deciding what the question calls for, outline your answer briefly before writing it on the exam paper.

Study habits are needed in addition to specific skills and methods of studying. For example, the child should develop the habit of concentrating. Before beginning to study he should try to put all other thoughts out of his mind. If he is bothered by a problem, he should attempt to settle it or resolve it in his mind so he can concentrate. Establishing particular questions to answer will also aid concentration. Another aid to improving concentration is to set a time limit for studying. Children usually get more done when they are pressed for time. Finally, some children will concentrate more effectively if they know they are going to be rewarded in some way for doing the assignment well.

Your child should have a specific *time to study.* Studying is usually more effective when the child knows he is going to study. If you must argue with your child to get him to study, concentration will be more difficult. Establish a study time that seems appropriate for your child. Some children are able to study most effectively immediately after school. Other children are ready for physical rather than study-type activities after school and would prefer to study in the evening. Your child may want to study in the morning before school begins. Work out the best time with your child so you do not have to nag him about studying.

You can aid your child by providing a *place to study*. Some children say they can study anywhere, but studying is most effective when all the supplies are available and when the atmosphere is conducive to concentration. Determine a place in your home for your child to study. It is easy to make a desk or buy an old desk and have fun painting and fixing it. Gather or purchase supplies and equipment such as a ruler, crayons, pencils, paper, glue, reference books, and a desk lamp. Plan the study area with your child and include some of his suggestions. Keep in mind this study area should be (1) free from distractions, (2) have appropriate lighting and (3) be comfortable for the child.

Reference Skills

We are living in an age of knowledge proliferation. Presently knowledge doubles every eight to ten years. At this rate it is impossible for a child to learn everything. Even the specialist finds it impossible to keep up to date in a very specialized field. The need to "look it up" becomes greater each year, so it is extremely important that your child *learn to locate and use books* effectively.

Many skills are involved in locating and using books and other *reference* materials. Some of the skills were explained in Chapter Four in the section on how to use the dictionary. Ideas on how to help your child learn alphabetical order, guide words, and a pronunciation key were presented. These same skills are also needed to use encyclopedias and other reference materials.

At the kindergarten and first grade level children must learn how to handle books properly and to find a specified page. Knowledge of and skills in using the different parts of the book, such as the preface, table of contents, index, bibliography, and appendix are also taught at the elementary school level. Elementary age children must also learn to use cross listings and identify key words.

The types of information found in encyclopedias, atlases, almanacs, and dictionaries seem common to us, but are foreign to the young child. The use of the card catalogue and other library aids must also be learned. All of these skills are introduced at the elementary school level.

As you can see, many complex skills are involved. If children do not master these, "looking something up" becomes an unpleasant chore. The individualized help that a parent can provide is needed again.

As you child *reads in different subject areas he needs some additional reading skills.* Every content area has a *specialized vocabulary* that must be understood. Your child must be able to read words such as add, change, double, hundred, remainder, and take away, to be successful in mathematics. In social studies words such as Eskimo, silo, citrus, delta, and irrigation are encountered. Scientific terms, for example, hibernate, vacuum, fertilizer, and atmosphere are found in elementary school textbooks. The list is endless! It is no wonder children have difficulty reading in some subject areas. This is especially true if the words are entirely new to them — that is, not a part of their listening or speaking vocabularies.

In addition to the new words, there are many symbols to learn. Remember the definition of reading indicates that reading is the interpretation of printed *symbols,* not just words. Mathematics involves using the symbols for addition, subtraction, multiplication, division, cents, degrees, and much more. There are also Roman numerals.

Maps and globes require special reading skills as do tables, graphs, and diagrams. Your child will see these frequently in the social studies and science books. He will be able to get more information if he is able to read these special ways of presenting material.

The importance of parents as partners with the school is readily seen. Children frequently ask for help with homework. You can understand why help is necessary when you consider all the skills and knowledge that must be used. The games, ideas, and activities in this chapter will help you as you help your child become a *student.*

Study Skills and Habits

*297bc. *SQ3R.* One of the best ways to help your child learn the SQ3R method is to go through the steps with him. Sometime when he has a reading assignment in social studies, health, or science, say, "Let's do it together." Begin by saying, "Let's find out what we are going to be reading before we read it," and proceed by going over the pictures, major headings, and summary. Next you might say, "It is a good idea to make up questions to answer so we can test each other." Show him how to change the major topics to questions. Have the child read each section of the assignment and then see if he can recite the questions. Finally, you might use a little game to review the assignment. A possible game is King of the Mountain. Ask the child certain questions to see if he can climb the mountain to be king. He is king if he can answer a specified number of questions.

*298bc. *Why.* When your child has a particular assignment make sure he knows the purpose of the assignment. You might say, "Why are you learning that?" Ask him for examples of when the new knowledge or skill will be useful. When he knows what to do and why he is doing it, set a time limit to increase his concentration. A reward can also be used to motivate the child.

299bc. *Memorizing.* If your child is required to memorize a selection, make sure he understands what it means. After he knows what he is memorizing, work on one line at a time, emphasizing meaningful phrases. Then work on the second line. Continue this procedure until the child knows the selection by heart.

*300bc. *A Thousand Words.* Many of the newer textbooks have beautiful illustrations which can help the child understand concepts. Ask your child questions about the pictures or simply point out some of the features which he may not have noticed. If you show some interest, your child will show more interest.

The need to "look it up" becomes greater every year, so it is important that children learn to use reference books effectively.

301c. *Stump Me.* After your child has read a particular assignment, ask him to make up questions to stump you. Children usually enjoy knowing something that adults do not know. By asking questions the child will be reinforcing his knowledge and organizing his thoughts.

*302abc. *Can He Do It?* Make sure your child is *able* to read his textbooks before you force him to read them. Many textbooks in social studies, health, and science are actually written above the grade level in which they are used. If your child misses more than one or two words in twenty, or fails to understand what he is reading, talk with his teacher to see what suggestions she has. Remember, children are not expected to read materials which are at their frustrational reading level. Perhaps she will ask you to read the assignments to your child. Often children can *listen* and understand what they cannot read and understand.

*303abc. *One Hundred Percent.* When your child gets test papers back you might tell him the correct answers for the ones he has missed. At the same time emphasize what he did correctly. You have opportunities to reteach what many teachers have not time to do. Keep in mind that the main reason for giving tests is to determine what the child has learned and what he still needs to learn. Remember, do not criticize or be impatient.

304c. *True/False.* After your child has read an assignment ask him some true/false questions. If the statement is false, have the child make it true. Keep score and give him a special treat if he answers most of the questions correctly.

305c. *Glance and Tell.* After your child has read a portion of a textbook, ask him to glance at a heading and see if he can tell you something about it. For example, if the heading is, "The Habits of Birds," ask him to recall some specific habits.

*306c. *Doing Reports.* When your child is first learning to do reports, do one with him. Begin by asking him what he wants to find out about the person, place, or event. For example, if his report is on George Washington, ask him what he wants to know about George Washington. Perhaps he will want to know when he was born, what he was like as a boy, what he did for the United States, and what other people thought about him. After questions are formulated, aid the child in selecting key words and reference materials to find the information. If the material is too difficult, feel free to read it to him.

307c. *Taking Notes.* Your child can take notes from his reading by using the simple outline form mentioned earlier. Show him how to write the main topic and list supporting details under it. The activities suggested in Chapter Five for noting the main ideas and details may be helpful. An example that is closely related to the child's life is also valuable. For example, you might show him the following:

A. We have a happy family. (Main Idea)
  1. We have fun together at the beach. (Detail)
  2. We help each other by doing certain jobs. (Detail)
  3. We say nice things to each other. (Detail)

*308c. *Writing Reports.* When a report is to be written show the child how to arrange the information for it. Include an introduction, body, and conclusion. Help him learn to write paragraphs by using topic sentences followed by sentences with supporting details. Explain again that writers usually make a rough copy and then recopy and proofread it.

*309c. *Oral Reports.* If your child has to give an oral report, show him how to make a note card so he will not have to read the entire report. Write key words to remind him of the details. He may want to tape the report and then evaluate it. You can show him the importance of gestures which will help to keep the attention of the audience. If he is really enthusiastic, he might want to make a poster, a picture, or a model with which to demonstrate his report.

Reference Skills

*310a. *Let's Look at My Books.* Even during the preschool years children are interested in encyclopedias. Of course they cannot read, but the pictures are interesting. If your child finds an insect, show him pictures of different insects in an encyclopedia. This will not only be informative, but will also help the child learn what kinds of information can be found in encyclopedias. Positive attitudes and habits can be formed during preschool and early school years by simply using the beautiful pictures in encyclopedias.

311bc. *The Largest City.* Ask your child to find the populations of the cities of his favorite baseball or football teams. An almanac or encyclopedia can be used. In addition to populations, he may want to learn more about the cities.

*312bc. *Glossaries.* Many textbooks include a glossary. Children usually prefer using it instead of the dictionary, since the number of words is limited and it is easier to find a particular word. After your child has read a section in a textbook, ask him if he looked for definitions of italicized words. If not, do this together to make him realize the value of using a glossary. Remember to refer back to the word and determine how it is used in context so you can select the appropriate meaning.

*313bc. *What's in an Atlas?* An atlas can be fascinating for children. You might plan a trip or compare the terrain of different parts of the world. Look at the different kinds of maps such as those showing products or population. Suggested activities using maps and globes are included in the next section of this chapter.

*314abc. *Let's Find Out.* Topics such as insects, planets, plants, animals, or events may come up as you are watching television or working in the yard. For example, if your child says, "How do TV pictures get into our house?" you can find out together by using encyclopedias. As mentioned earlier, there are many skills involved in using the encyclopedia, so it is wise to help your child. Often parents complain because they have spent a lot of money on a set of encyclopedias that their child never uses. But remember, it is necessary to show your child how to use it! As you locate information "think out loud," so your child will realize why you select a certain volume of an encyclopedia. Point out cross references and other aids, such as the index.

*315b. *Front of the Book.* When you are using books with your child, help him develop the habit of looking at the table of contents to get an idea of what the book is about. This is especially useful when skimming a book to see if it has the information he wants. He might also develop the habit of reading the preface to learn about the purpose of the book. Again your task is to make your child aware of the many aids which are included in books.

316c. *Let Your Fingers Do the Thumbing.* Skill in using an index saves time. Most elementary school textbooks provide an index so children can locate particular topics quickly. Glance at the index in one of your child's books and then ask him questions, such as on what page he would find out about the Spanish-American War. Set a time limit of one or two minutes to locate the correct page. The newspaper can also be used for the activity since it has an index. Ask your child the page number for sports, movies, and comics.

*317abc. *Selecting Reference Books.* When purchasing reference materials for your child, have him read selections which interest him to get an idea whether the reading level is appropriate. Also look at the durability of the volumes, check to see that they lie flat when open, and that print does not show through from the other side. I believe that the number and quality of illustrations is also an important criterion. Provide all different types of reference materials including almanacs, atlases, dictionaries, and books on specific topics such as weather, human body, or shells. See Appendix H for suggested reference materials. Survey many before purchasing.

318abc. *Just for Fun.* Children like to look at encyclopedias without having a specific assignment. Some families give each person a volume to skim. Then each family member selects a topic or picture and tells the others about it. Some topics children especially enjoy are: the human body or particular parts of the body, animals, insects, plants, flags, and means of transportation.

319bc. *My Book.* One of the best activities for helping your child learn about the various parts of a book is to actually make a book. Select a favorite topic and then find pictures and write sentences or paragraphs concerning the topics. Have the child make a title page, a table of contents, and a list of pictures or illustrations.

*320bc. *Appendices.* Help your child realize the value of using appendices. Explain that often authors list information in these appendices so readers can refer to it quickly. Look at the appendices together. If there are charts show your child how to use them. Point out the tables of facts often found in math books and discuss when the child might refer to these. Your child will get "more mileage" from his book if you help him become aware of all the resources usually included in books.

*321bc. *Key Words.* Your child may encounter difficulty when locating material if he is not able to note the key words. As you look for information together, emphasize the *key words* which help you find the information you want. For example, if your child is interested in learning more about poisonous snakes commonly found in North America, you must help him realize that the key word is "snakes," rather than "poisonous" or "North America." If the entry is not listed under snakes, tell your child you must now look under reptiles since snakes are reptiles. *Talk* about your reasons for selecting certain key words and consequently certain parts of a book or volumes of an encyclopedia.

322c. *Easy to Find.* The best way for your child to learn how to use a card catalogue is to actually go to the library in pursuit of some topic or book by a particular author. If you work with him a few times, he will soon be able to use the card catalogue and will realize the value of it. Point out the three different types of cards — subject, author, and title — and ask him why we have all three kinds. Show him how he can find all the books about one of his special interests by using the subject cards. If he likes books by a particular author, have him look for the author cards. Check to see if your library has special classes to help children develop this and other library skills.

323c. *Fascinating Facts.* Most intermediate grade children enjoy reading unusual facts. The almanac is an excellent source since it has facts about almost any topic. Purchase an almanac for your child and read some of the interesting facts to him. Unusual facts are also found in the *Guinness Book of World Records* by Norris McWhirter and Ross McWhirter. Before you know it, he will be reading many of the facts to you.

Specialized Reading Skills in Subject Areas

324ab. *My Neighborhood.* Your child might enjoy making a map of his room or neighborhood. This is the first step in learning to read maps. Help him draw a simple diagram of the house or neighborhood. He will soon realize the importance of using symbols.

325ab. *Symbol or Number Concentration.* You can help your child learn symbols and/or numbers by having him match words and the symbols which represent them or numerals and words. Use 3 x 5 index cards and write the symbol on one card and the word on another card. For example, you may write "+" on one card and "plus" on another card. Make as many pairs as necessary using the symbols your child is learning. Place the cards face down on the table and take turns turning over two cards. If the symbol and word match, the player keeps the pairs of cards and gets another turn. If not, the two cards are turned over and the next player has a turn. The player with the most cards at the end of the game is the winner. Some symbols and numerals commonly found in elementary school textbooks are as follows:

Numerals:

1	one	2	two	3	three	4	four
5	five	6	six	7	seven	8	eight
9	nine	10	ten	11	eleven	12	twelve
		100	one hundred	1000	one thousand		

Symbols:

=	equals	+	plus	—	minus	×	times
>	greater than	°	degrees	<	less than	'	feet
"	inches						

326ab. *Typing Symbols.* If your child has difficulty remembering such symbols as: +, —, %, ×, ¢, and #, have him type a row of each symbol. As he types the symbols, he should say them aloud. When he has a row of each one, ask him to cut the paper into strips. Then ask him for a particular symbol. Have him point them out as he sees them in his daily activities.

*327bc. *3S-D for Specialized Vocabulary.* Your child can pronounce unknown words by using a formula called 3S-D. The first S stands for "*s*ound it out," the second S for look at the "*s*tructure of the word," and the third S means read the "rest of the *s*entence" to see if you can get the meaning of the word. The D stands for *d*ictionary which can be consulted for pronunciation and meaning of a new word. As your child is reading and encounters specialized words in his content books, ask him to apply this formula.

*328bc. *Keys to Math.* When your child is reading story problems in math, ask him to look for key words such as sold, added, received, lost or take away. Soon he will understand that these specialized vocabulary words tell him what process to use. Go over a page of problems and have him tell you what he has to do to find the answer. Ask him to apply the SQFP2C formula when doing problems which are presented in paragraph form. Each letter of the formula represents a step your child should follow.

S — *Survey* the problem to get a general idea of it.

Q — Determine what *question* is asked.

F — Read to find the most important *facts.*

P — Decide what *process(es)* to use — addition, multiplication, and so forth.

C — Do the *computation.*

C — Ask yourself if the answer makes sense and use the appropriate *checking* method.

329bc. *Can You Find?* A road map of your city or area will help your child develop map skills. Locate your house and then have the child find a nearby point of interest by using the index. If your child has difficulty, show him the point of interest and then have him notice the guide letters and numbers on the side of the map. You might have him figure out the distance from your house to the point of interest by using the scale.

330bc. *Salt Maps.* Make a salt and flour map by following these directions:

Make a dough with 2 cups of flour, one cup of salt, and one cup of water.

Outline the map. Mold the mixture to show desired features.

Color the different features with cold water paints.

(Use less salt on damp days or in regions where the humidity is high, since salt absorbs water from the atmosphere.)

331bc. *Road Maps.* Road maps are usually free and make excellent teaching devices. Get a map and glue it to a piece of posterboard. Then have your child cut out the different states or counties to make a puzzle of the map. Time him to see how quickly he can put it together. In doing so, have him notice the special symbols, scale, and index.

332bc. *Which Way?* As you are taking a trip to the store or some other place, ask your child to give you directions. Help him use east, west, north, and south as he describes the route. You can vary this activity by giving your child directions and see if he can guess where you are taking him.

333c. *Wood Burning Maps.* Your child may enjoy tracing the outline of a map on a piece of wood. He can then wood-burn the outline and add points of interest. Children are usually very proud of these special efforts even though they require time to make.

334c. *Vacations Are Fun!* When you are going on a vacation in an automobile, ask your child to be the co-pilot. He can read the travel books and tourist brochures to point out the places of interest and how many miles to the next town. Of course, half the fun of a vacation is the anticipation. Sit down with your child before the trip and plan the best route. You can also use encyclopedias to learn more about the points of interest.

335c. *Tracing.* Elementary school age children enjoy tracing maps and diagrams. In doing so they are learning to read them. Provide onion skin or tracing paper so your child can make his own maps and diagrams. After tracing, he can label the different parts of the diagram or color the maps.

336c. *Map Time Find.* Ask your child to find a particular place on the map as quickly as possible. He will see the advantage of using the index to the map and latitude and longitude figures for finding unfamiliar places. Keep a record of the time it takes to find a particular place so the child can notice his progress.

337c. *Abbreviations for States.* Help your child learn abbreviations in different subject areas. In social studies children are usually required to learn the abbreviations for states. Have your child trace a map of the whole country and then write the abbreviations for the different states.

The two-letter abbreviations which are approved by the Post Office for the United States are:

Alabama	AL	Dist. of Col.	DC
Alaska	AK	Florida	FL
Arizona	AZ	Georgia	GA
Arkansas	AR	Guam	GU
California	CA	Hawaii	HI
Colorado	CO	Idaho	ID
Connecticut	CT	Illinois	IL
Delaware	DE	Indiana	IN

Iowa	IA	North Dakota	ND
Kansas	KS	Ohio	OH
Kentucky	KY	Oklahoma	OK
Louisiana	LA	Oregon	OR
Maine	ME	Pennsylvania	PA
Maryland	MD	Puerto Rico	PR
Massachusetts	MA	Rhode Island	RI
Michigan	MI	South Carolina	SC
Minnesota	MN	South Dakota	SD
Mississippi	MS	Tennessee	TN
Missouri	MO	Texas	TX
Montana	MT	Utah	UT
Nebraska	NE	Vermont	VT
Nevada	NV	Virginia	VA
New Hampshire	NH	Virgin Islands	VI
New Jersey	NJ	Washington	WA
New Mexico	NM	West Virginia	WV
New York	NY	Wisconsin	WI
North Carolina	NC	Wyoming	WY

338c. *Great Graphs.* Children usually enjoy making bar graphs of temperature, rainfall, baseball standings, or population. The local newspaper can be used to provide information. Circle graphs can be made of the child's daily program. For example, he might indicate the hours he is in school, at sleep, at play, or eating. Talk with your child about why we have graphs. Have him realize that graphs are used to present information in picture form to make it easier to see relationships and remember important facts.

339c. *Interest Scrapbook.* Some children enjoy making scrapbooks of newspaper clippings of particular events or topics. Perhaps your child would like to make a scrapbook of some baseball team, political leader, or unusual event.

340c. *Papier-mâché Maps.* Children usually enjoy working with papier-mâché. Since this is a messy activity for the classroom, many teachers do not use it as frequently as they would like to. The home is a perfect place for the child to make maps and other objects of papier-mâché. Use the following directions:

a. Tear newspaper into small bits, soak overnight to soften.
b. Beat into a soft pulp with a spoon, draining off excess water.
c. Add 4 tablespoons of paste to each quart of paper pulp. Make the paste with flour by slowly adding water to make it creamy. Heat at a low temperature for 5 minutes and stir. Add cold water if it is too thick. You may want to add oil of wintergreen drops to prevent spoiling. Mix thoroughly.
d. Trace the outline of the area to be shown on heavy cardboard.
e. Mold the paper pulp within the outline to show the desired elevations.
f. Dry thoroughly, paint, and cover with colorless shellac when paint is dry.

A fascination for books and reading can be instilled in children at a very early age.

CHAPTER NINE

HOW TO HELP YOUR CHILD DEVELOP INTEREST IN READING

Some children express little or no interest in reading, even though they can read. Many parents complain that they just cannot get their child to read. The child enjoys watching television or playing, but will not sit down to read a book. I am sure most children go through a stage when reading is not as popular as other activities. At the same time, I understand why parents who have found pleasure and knowledge from reading are concerned when their children do not read.

One of the first questions I ask when talking to concerned parents is, "Does the child have books and magazines that are of interest to him and that he is capable of reading?" Children must have a reason for reading — for enjoyment or information — before they are going to read. Also, the books must be at the appropriate level. We all avoid doing those things we cannot do well and/or do not find interesting. The child who has books that are too difficult or uninteresting will not read them.

Another question I ask is if the parents read. Children must value reading before they will read. Values are taught by parents' actions, rather than words. If you read, then your child will see that reading is a worthwhile activity.

Finally, I ask the concerned parents if there is time provided for reading. By this I do not mean that a specified period of time should be established every day. Rather, is the television set ever turned off so the child has free time? It is common today for children to have some special activities every night or have a series of television programs to watch throughout the entire evening. This can be good in moderation, but the child must also have free time for thinking, creating, and reading. Parents have the responsibility to see that their children have free time.

Use the following checklist as you think about your child's interests. When you are fully aware of the things your child likes, and have talked with his teacher to determine his reading levels, visit the library or local bookstore with your child. Share this information with the librarian or buyer of children's books and you will soon get materials that will "turn your child on" to reading.

—— Fairy tales and make believe stories
—— Cars, trucks, jets, trains
—— Cowboys and Indians
—— Finger painting or working with leather, clay, or a wood burner
—— Sewing or weaving
—— Sports — football, baseball, soccer, bowling, swimming
—— Bicycle riding, go-carts, roller skating
—— Puppets, drama
—— Dolls
—— Scientific objects — magnets, insects, plants, machines, chemicals
—— Making jewelry
—— Animals — pets, horses, reptiles
—— Music — songs, instruments
—— Comics, jokes, and riddles
—— Mystery stories or scary shows
—— Famous people — heroes or heroines
—— Collecting shells, rocks, stamps, or coins
—— Making wood products — book ends, puzzles, dog houses
—— Cooking
—— Gardening — growing food or flowers

If you find your child seems to lack interest in reading, try these ideas and activities to increase his interest. Remember, changes in attitudes do not take place overnight — be patient and tolerant.

Developing Interest in Reading

341bc. *The "Mad" Scientist.* If your child is interested in science, consider purchasing a chemistry set for him. A book of experiments is usually included with the set. This will help your child see the value of reading and develop his skill in following written directions. Other scientific hobbies, such as astronomy, electronics, and meteorology, provide opportunities for reading because there are so many good books available. Capitalize on your child's interests by describing them to the librarian or the buyer of children's books at your local bookstore. They will be able to suggest many books at appropriate levels. Remember to take your child with you so he can help with the selection process.

342bc. *Making Models.* Written directions are usually included for models children put together. Many children like to assemble ships, automobiles, and airplanes. Models of the different parts of the human body are available too. Your child can have fun as he is reading.

343bc. *How To.* Many "how to" books are available for doing such things as binding books, repairing appliances, knitting, sewing, and playing sports. If your child is interested in learning any of these new skills,

130

you might purchase a book for him or borrow one from the library. If he is unable to read it, read it to him. It will help him see the value of books.

344bc. *Music and Reading.* Written music for playing many instruments such as piano, organ, guitar, and banjo can motivate the child to read more. Sometimes children learn to play by letter, and the words of the song are often included. Again, reading can be useful as well as fun.

345bc. *Pets.* There are many good books available on how to care for cats, tropical fish, birds, dogs, hamsters, and rabbits. If your child has a pet, obtain books describing more about it and its habits.

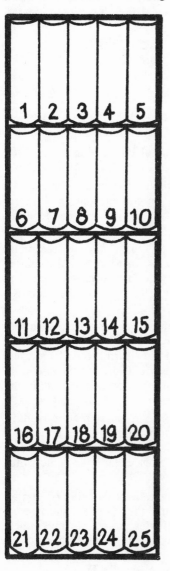

346bc. *Collections.* Your child probably has some collections. These can be used to increase interest in reading. When a child collects and labels stamps, coins, rocks, shells, insects, leaves, autographs, china, or souvenirs, reading is necessary. There are many good books available for collectors.

347bc. *Sports.* Nearly every sport provides opportunities for reading. There are football programs, baseball cards, and directions on how to develop proficiency at different sports. In addition, newspapers and magazines include information about different games and the heroes and heroines of the games. Obtain material that interests your child.

348abc. *Thin Books.* If your child is hesitant about reading, begin by having him select very short books. Children get a sense of accomplishment when they complete a book. Your child will be happier if he can complete ten short books rather than one long one. Ask a librarian or the child's teacher for some interesting thin books.

349ab. *My Bookcase.* Children enjoy keeping track of what they have done. You can have your child keep a record of the books he has read by drawing a miniature bookcase and writing the title on each "book." See if he can complete a bookcase of twenty-five small books. See illustration.

Another way of keeping a record of books the child has read is to make a bookworm or a train. Make a separate section or car for each book. He can write the name of the book and the author. Display them in his room and see how long he can make the worm or train.

*350abc. *Book Clubs.* There are some paperback book clubs children can join without having to buy a set number of books per year. Your child's teacher should be able to provide information on appropriate book clubs for your child. If not, write to Scholastic Magazines and Book Service, which is listed in Appendix D. Your child will look forward to books arriving in the mail. The wait after ordering a book makes it more exciting.

351c. *High Interest - Low Vocabulary.* There are many high interest - low vocabulary books available for older children who are reading at low levels. Ask the librarian or your child's teacher if they have any. Some of the favorite series are:

The Checkered Flag Series (cars, racing, motorcycles)
Jim Forest Readers
Morgan Bay Mysteries
Deep Sea Adventures
Wildlife Adventure Series

For more information, write to Field Educational Publications, Inc., 2400 Hanover Street, Palo Alto, California 94304.

*352abc. *Tried and True.* One sure method of increasing interest is to read to your child. He will see that books do contain many adventures and ideas. Elementary school children are never too old to listen to exciting stories or interesting information.

353bc. *Brochures.* Your child may want to send for some free or inexpensive brochures. Most states have brochures for tourists and are more than willing to send very attractive reading material. Teach your child to write letters to request free materials or simply clip and mail the advertisements which are often found in adult magazines.

354bc. *Comics.* There are some good comic books children seem naturally motivated to read. Also, the comics in daily and Sunday newspapers are attractive to children. Your child can learn words from these sources as well as from textbooks. The *Electric Company* is also publishing comic books designed to help children learn particular sounds and generalizations concerning phonics. See Appendix D for the address.

355bc. *Read the Directions.* Many games children play require reading. For example, one must read cards in Monopoly, and numbers and words in Sorry. You do not need to be concerned if your child is not reading books all the time. Many of these other materials include the same words he would be reading in books.

*356abc. *Marvelous Magazines.* Magazines were mentioned earlier as a source of reading material. The fact that they contain short selections, cartoons and jokes, and interesting activities and games make them attractive to children. Purchase some magazines at a newsstand to see which ones particularly interest your child. A subscription would be very valuable to him. Suggestions can be found in Appendix D.

*357abc. *Do You Know What, Mom?* Show your child that you are sincerely interested in what he is reading. This does not mean that you pressure him to tell you everything about the reading material, but rather that you are ready to listen and praise him for the ideas that he wants to share.

*358abc. *Springboard.* Television programs can serve as a springboard to reading. There will be animals, countries, and events that the child wants to know more about. Good books or appropriate encyclopedias should be made available.

*359abc. *Don't Forget the Books.* In traveling you would be wise to take along some magazines, comic books, or other books. While riding in a car the child may have "nothing better to do." This opportunity may help him see that reading can be valuable and is fun.

360c. *Dream Cars.* If your child is interested in cars, use magazines to clip pictures showing the different models. Your child may enjoy making his own scrapbook by cutting out pictures of models and writing the names and/or descriptions of them.

361c. *Home Movies.* Your child may enjoy writing descriptions for photographs or scripts for slides and movies you have taken. This is the language experience approach, because the child is writing or dictating his own stories. If your child is not able to write the words, you might write them and then help him read the scripts as he shows the pictures.

362c. *Current Events.* There are many valuable articles in the newspaper of interest to children. In addition to news articles, weather charts, astrology charts, and advertisements appeal to children. Current events papers written at your child's level are available. I recommend *My Weekly Reader* which is listed in Appendix D.

363bc. *Scouts.* Girl scout or boy scout guides usually include excellent reading material. Sunday school papers, and other club publications are also interesting. Please keep in mind that any material will do to help your child learn to read, if it is written at his level.

364bc. *If You . . . I'll . . .* Rewards are important if your child is really turned off by reading. Once you have determined that he is interested in a particular book and is capable of reading it, offer him a reward, such as going bowling, having a special dessert, or some other reasonable reward. Never punish him for not reading. Punishment will increase his dislike of reading.

365bc. *Wider Horizons.* If you would like to help your child expand his interests in reading, make a chart for different categories of books. Possible categories are: adventure, animal stories, fairy tales, poetry, science, sports, travel, inventions or machines, biographies, and humor. Your child can keep a record to see if he is reading in all categories. Each time he finishes reading a book, he may color one square in the row opposite the type of book. Use different colors for each type. See drawing on page 134.

My Reading Chart

KIND OF BOOK	1	2	3	4	5	6	7	8	9
Adventure									
Animal Stories									
Fairy Tales									
Fiction									
Poetry									
Science									
Just For Fun									
Sports									

366abc. *Associations.* Throughout this book I have encouraged you to take your child to the local library or bookstore. I recommend this highly because I believe librarians and the buyers of children's books are your most up-to-date sources of information concerning books appropriate for your child's interests and reading level. If your child does not seem too enthralled about visiting the library and bookstore, try to make the trip more pleasant by stopping for a treat on the way home. A milkshake, an ice cream cone, or a few minutes at a park or playground can help your child form pleasant associations with visiting the library or bookstore. This may sound like a bribe, and perhaps it is, but it has worked for many parents.

*367abc. *Certificate of Success.* When your child has read a certain number of books, write his name on the Award Certificate (pages 187-191). This will be more attractive if you mount it on colored cardboard and show it to others.

368abc. *Writing Stories about Your Child.* You may want to write some stories about your child which portray his strengths or make him the main character in an exciting adventure. For example, I wrote the following about my children:

JIMMY AND JENNIFER SAVE A CHILD

One day Jimmy and Jennifer went swimming. They had fun playing in the sand. Soon they heard someone shout, "Help!" They saw a child was in trouble.

Jennifer ran to tell the lifeguard. Jimmy started to swim to save the child. Soon the lifeguard came running. He went into the water to save the child.

The lifeguard brought the child out of the water. Jimmy and Jennifer helped the other people stand back. Soon the child was fine.

The lifeguard gave Jimmy and Jennifer an award for helping. The child's mom bought them a treat. Everyone told Jimmy and Jennifer how brave they were. It was an exciting day because Jimmy and Jennifer helped save a child's life.

After writing the story, you can determine its reading level by using the graph for *Estimating Readability* which follows. This graph was developed by Edward Fry to find out the reading levels of written materials. Follow these instructions when using the graph:

a. Count 100 words in the story, skipping all proper nouns, dates, and numerals. Make sure you begin counting at the beginning of a sentence. Do not count the words in a title. Your story may be more than 100 words, but a 100-word sample is sufficient for determining its readability.

b. Count the number of sentences in the 100-word selection. If the final sentence does not end at the end of your 100 words, determine what proportion of it you are including in the 100-word count. Estimate the last sentence to the nearest tenth. For example, if the final sentence in a 100-word count has 16 words, and eight of these are in the 100-word count, the final sentence would be counted as .5 sentences.

c. Count the number of syllables in the 100-word passage. For example: though — 1 syllable, counted — 2 syllables, determine — 3 syllables, appropriate — 4 syllables. Keep in mind there will be a syllable for each vowel sound heard when a word is pronounced. Remember, proper nouns, dates, and numerals are not counted.

d. Refer to Fry's graph. Notice the grid of intersecting lines. The vertical lines represent average number of syllables per 100 words. The horizontal lines represent the average number of sentences per 100 words. Where any two intersecting vertical and horizontal lines meet, approximate grade levels are revealed. Record the approximate grade level of the selection at this time. According to Fry, most of the intersecting points will fall near the curved line. If the intersecting point should fall in the gray area, conclude that the results are invalid.

e. Remember this is an estimate of readability. Fry states that the estimates are probably within one year of the true estimate of readability.

Let's apply these directions to the story written above. First, we count 100 words skipping all proper nouns (Jimmy, Jennifer, and any other particular nouns which begin with capital letters). We also skip numerals (1, 2, 3) unless they are in written form (one, two, three). In the story, "Jimmy and Jennifer Save a Child," the 100th word is "because" which is in the last sentence.

GRAPH FOR ESTIMATING READABILITY

by Edward Fry, Rutgers University Reading Center, New Jersey

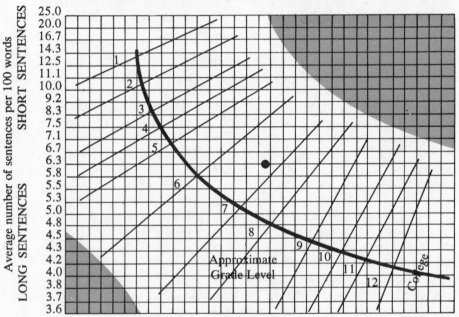

Average number of syllables per 100 words

DIRECTIONS: Randomly select three one-hundred word passages from a book or an article. Plot average number of syllables and average number of sentences per 100 words on graph to determine the grade level of the material. Choose more passages per book if great variability is observed and conclude that the book has uneven readability. Few books will fall in gray area, but when they do grade level scores are invalid.

		Syllables	Sentences
EXAMPLE:	1st Hundred Words	124	6.6
	2nd Hundred Words	141	5.5
	3rd Hundred Words	158	6.8
	AVERAGE	141	6.3

READABILITY 7th GRADE (see dot plotted on graph)

There are 14 complete sentences. In addition 6 of the 12 words (excluding proper nouns) in the last sentence are included in our 100-word sample; thus, this equals one half or .5 of a sentence. In total we have 14.5 sentences.

The easiest way to count syllables is by reading the story out loud and putting a slash over each syllable you hear. Remember, a syllable is a sound unit in a word. Notice we have 122 syllables in the 100 words of this story. Again we skip proper nouns and numerals when counting syllables.

One day Jimmy and Jennifer went swimming. They had fun playing in the sand. Soon they heard someone shout, "Help!" They saw a child was in trouble.

Jennifer ran to tell the lifeguard. Jimmy started to swim to save the child. Soon the lifeguard came running. He went into the water to save the child.

The lifeguard brought the child out of the water. Jimmy and Jennifer helped the other people stand back. Soon the child was fine.

The lifeguard gave Jimmy and Jennifer an award for helping. The child's mom bought them a treat. Everyone told Jimmy and Jennifer how brave they were. It was an exciting day because /100 words/ Jimmy and Jennifer helped save a child's life.

In referring to Fry's graph, locate the 122 syllables at the top of the graph and 14.5 sentences. Follow the line down and across; where the points intersect, notice the grade level band. In this sample, the estimate of readability is between first and second grade. Remember the estimate may vary within one year of the true estimate of readability; thus, the estimate of readability for this selection is high first or second grade.

If you write a story which is too difficult for your child to read, you can lower the reading level by *increasing* the number of sentences (make shorter sentences). Another way to lower the reading level is to decrease the number of syllables, i.e., substitute one-syllable words for multi-syllable words.

I realize this activity requires time, but the dividends you get — a child who wants to read a personalized story — makes every minute spent on it worthwhile.

369abc. *Another Use of Fry's Graph.* Fry's graph can also be used to determine the reading levels of books. If you have books which concern your child's interests, and wonder if the reading level is suitable for him, follow the directions which are listed under Fry's graph. By doing so you will be taking into consideration the two most important factors which influence a child's desire to read: (a) whether or not the material is *interesting* and (b) whether or not the *reading level is appropriate.*

CHAPTER TEN

WHEN YOUR CHILD NEEDS SPECIALIZED HELP

All parents hope that their child will not have difficulty learning to read. The fact is though, many children do not learn to read as well as expected. Some children are behind when they enter school, while others do not make normal progress during the school years. The reading disability may be mild, moderate, or severe, depending upon the child's *expected* reading level.

One way of estimating the expected reading level is by multiplying the number of years the child has been in school by his IQ and then adding 1.0. The 1.0 is added because his grade placement when he entered school was 1.0. For example, a child with an IQ of 105 who has completed 4½ years of school (half way through the fifth grade) is expected to read at the 5.7 grade level (fifth grade, seventh month).

Most reading specialists believe a child who is reading *two years below his expected reading level* needs remedial reading instruction. Such instruction usually takes place in a special reading class in the school and/ or a private reading clinic or tutor. If the child's reading level is less than two years below his expected level, he needs corrective reading instruction. Classroom teachers usually are responsible for corrective reading programs.

Causes of Reading Failure

There are many reasons why some children fail to achieve their expected reading level. Usually two or more factors operate together to hinder progress. Eight of the major factors which influence achievement in reading are discussed below. As you read these factors, try to determine the factors that are helping your child succeed, as well as those that may be hindering his progress.

Health

Your child's general health is an important factor. Reading is a highly abstract task requiring a great deal of concentration. The child who is tired, hungry, or who has some physical deficiency is likely to experience some difficulty in learning to read. Glandular disturbances and thyroid dysfunctions can hinder reading achievement because of fatigue. Unexpected childhood illnesses may cause extended absences from school. The importance of regular medical examinations, proper meals, and sufficient rest cannot be overemphasized. Remember, you are the provider for your child.

Auditory Skills

The importance of your child's listening and speaking vocabularies has been emphasized throughout this book. Auditory skills are essential for the development of listening and speaking vocabularies, which in turn influences the development of the reading vocabulary. One of the steps in the process of reading is relating the symbols to oral language and, if auditory skills have hindered the development of an adequate oral language, the child may experience difficulty in reading. Your child must be able to hear, distinguish, and remember sounds when learning to read. Observe your child to notice if he (a) cups his ear with his hand in order to hear you, (b) complains of persistent earaches and sore throats, (c) has difficulty in learning some speech sounds and words, (d) is inattentive when others are talking to him, and (e) has excessive drainage or inflammation of the ears.

Vision

Reading is a visual process—the child must perceive and decode printed symbols. In addition to obtaining a clear image of the symbols, your child must be able to remember symbols and follow lines of printed symbols. There is more to seeing than simply having 20/20 vision or excellent visual acuity. Observe your child to notice if he (a) loses his place frequently when reading, (b) becomes restless or irritable when doing close work, (c) rubs his eyes excessively, (d) uses one eye to focus, (e) has inflamed, watery, crossed, or swollen eyes frequently, (f) complains of nausea or dizziness following close work, (g) reverses many letters and words beyond the age of seven, and (h) stumbles frequently or seems awkward in his movements.

Educational Factors

Schools can also be a cause of reading failure. Teachers who are incompetent or have poor attitudes toward children and reading can hinder the child. If the materials and methods are not appropriate, your child will be bored or frustrated. Teachers who do not make reading instruction meaningful and exciting contribute to reading failure too. Talk to your child to see what kinds of things he is doing in school. Go over his papers with him to see if he has really learned what was expected of him. Listen to him read his school books to see if they are at his independent, instructional, or frustrational reading levels (see Chapter Five). Make an appointment to visit your child's teacher to observe or have a conference. Teachers generally welcome parents and are happy to explain their methods, materials, ways of grouping and scheduling the reading program, and provide other information which you may desire. Talk with the principal if you have questions the teacher cannot answer. Avoid going to the principal without having first talked to your child's teacher. Be ready to cooperate, remembering that the teacher has many children assigned to her in addition to your child.

Parental Causes

Consider the child who wakes up and hears his parents fighting every morning. Parents sometimes say unkind things to each other which worry the child. At the same time children usually get the brunt of the argument because the parents are angry and say unpleasant things. How can that child concentrate when he gets to school? There are other ways that parents cause reading problems. If parents do not provide the child with experiences and books, he is bound to have difficulty learning to read. Similarly, if the parents never read, the child is not going to learn the value of reading. The child who learns language patterns that are different from those usually found in textbooks may experience difficulty too.

Parents who put too much pressure on the child also cause reading problems. The parent who allows the child to stay up very late on school nights can expect the child to have difficulty in school and especially in reading where concentration is required. Parents can expect their child to fail in reading if they do not show interest in him. Those parents who have all the time in the world for many social engagements, but little or no time for their child, are as guilty as parents who put too much pressure on their child. Why should a child try to do his best when no one seems to care or when so much is expected of him that he never pleases others?

This is not to say that parents are expected to devote all of their time to their child. Parents also need to have a life of their own which includes activities with other adults. The parents who spend all of their time considering what the child needs and would like, generally spoil the child. This in turn can cause reading problems because the child cannot receive the same amount and degree of attention in the classroom. Make sure you have a life of your own in addition to fulfilling the responsibilities of a VIP. Remember, your major responsibilities are to (a) help your child *value* reading, (b) show *interest* in his reading achievement, and (c) *provide* books, experiences, and help the child develop physically, mentally and social-emotionally.

Aptitude for Reading

Intelligence, as measured by present day intelligence tests, correlates highly with success in reading. This high correlation is due to the fact

140

that many of the factors of intelligence which are measured by a typical intelligence test are the same factors required for success in reading. For example, most intelligence tests measure vocabulary, visual perception skills, general information, auditory memory, and the ability to use good judgment in solving problems. It is no wonder then that children who do poorly on intelligence tests also do poorly in reading. Research has indicated that IQ's can be raised by improving vocabulary, visual skills, and so forth.

Neurological functioning also seems to be related to aptitude for learning to read. There are some children who score average or above average IQ's and yet do not seem to have the ability to profit from reading instruction. During the past eight or ten years children with normal intelligence who have experienced difficulty in learning to read have been labeled "dyslexic." The term "dyslexia" has never been defined precisely. Most medical doctors and reading specialists raise their eyebrows when they hear the term because there is no one commonly accepted definition. It has been used to label those children who seem to have the intelligence, but are unable to process language symbols. Visual problems as evidenced by writing letters in reverse are usually associated with dyslexia; however, the term has been used as a blanket to cover many atypical behaviors.

The term which is more popular today for children with average intelligence and below average achievement in reading is "learning disabled." Children with normal intelligence who do not learn to read for unknown reasons are sometimes classified as having a learning disability. The disability is classified as a visual, auditory, and/or neurological learning disability, according to the characteristics or special abilities which seem to be deficient. At this time there are many theories which attempt to explain the causes of certain learning disabilities; however, there is not enough conclusive evidence to state any commonly accepted generalizations.

Brain damage as evidenced by poor motor coordination, or poor visual and auditory memory sometimes lowers the child's aptitude for learning to read. Physicians or reading specialists often will ask about the conditions at the time of the child's birth. They may also ask if the child has had any serious injuries or prolonged periods of high fever. It is still not known how many reading problems are caused by brain damage; however, brain damage does seem to affect aptitude for learning to read.

Observe your child over a long period of time to notice if he (a) is over-active when compared to other children his age and size, (b) quite awkward in running and walking, (c) complains of persistent headaches, (d) is easily distracted, (e) has difficulty remembering things, and (f) reverses many letters and words beyond the age of seven. Also, keep records of any head injuries or high fevers. Remember that all children are hyperactive when they are excited, have fevers when ill, and display many of the other symptoms which are mentioned above. Only be concerned when these behaviors occur frequently.

Language Factors

Children differ in language development just as they differ in height, weight, and color. Some children talk early, while others are slower to develop speaking skills. Language problems can cause difficulty when your child is pressured to perform tasks for which he is not ready. Some children simply are not ready for formal reading instruction at the age of five or six because they have been slower in developing the language skills which are prerequisites for reading.

As with other aspects of growth, language can develop in spurts. For example, some children seem to grow physically more rapidly one year than in another year. Similarly, some children develop more language skills in one year than in another year. Part of the readiness for speaking depends upon your child's maturation of speech organs and neuromuscular system. Growth in vocabulary and sentence length are related to the total development of the child. The importance of developing listening and speaking skills as prerequisites for learning to read were stressed in Chapter Two. The child who is forced to read before developing the prerequisite skills will encounter difficulty in learning to read.

Language development also influences reading in terms of the language patterns a child develops. If the sentence structure and vocabulary the child learns are different from those which are found in the textbooks he reads, he is likely to experience difficulty. Again the importance of your model of language — sentence structure, grammar, vocabulary — is realized.

Social-Emotional Factors

The final factor which influences reading achievement is social-emotional development. The child who does not get along with others and has a poor self-concept can experience difficulty in learning to read. Also, the child who does not cooperate with his teacher and his peers may miss out on reading instruction because he is not paying attention. The child who has a defeatist attitude as a result of constant criticism by parents and/or teachers generally has trouble in learning to read. Some children who are constantly compared to siblings who read well, avoid reading and look for other strengths they can develop. In general, the child who is happy with himself and can function well in group situations has a better chance of learning.

As you read these factors, did you ask yourself which ones are helping your child succeed? Which seem to be hindering his progress? You probably realize that these factors do not operate in isolation, but rather work together to help or hinder reading progress.

Sources of Help — Have Pals

If you did identify factors that will help your child succeed you now know the strengths on which you can build. You will need help from other specialists and friends to help your child overcome any factors that may be causing reading failure. The best advice that I can give you consists of two words which are made up from the first letter of each of the major factors which influence reading achievement:

> *H*ealth
> *A*uditory Skills
> *V*isual Skills
> *E*ducational Factors
> *P*arental Causes
> *A*ptitude
> *L*anguage
> *S*ocial

HAVE PALS! Being a parent is one of the most challenging, satisfying, and frustrating roles in life. It is challenging because each child is different. It is satisfying to love your child, receive love, and watch him grow. Rearing children can also be frustrating because you want your child to have the best and to be the best, but this is not always possible. There is no doubt about it — you must HAVE PALS!

The "pals" which are commonly available to you are listed below for each of the major factors that influence reading achievement. You can use this list to gather more information which will help you to help your child. I have tried to briefly outline the major services which are available from your pals. In general, you will notice that I have listed people who are available in the typical community. In addition, the addresses for some of the most helpful national agencies are provided. Many times there are local chapters of these agencies. Ask your pediatrician, child's teacher, principal, and/or school psychologist which agencies are available in your community. Read the list of pals carefully so you are aware of all the specialized help which is available for children who are experiencing difficulty.

Have Pals for Health Problems

a. Classroom Teacher — Observes symptoms of possible health problems and makes referrals to you and/or the school nurse.
b. School Nurse — Screens for possible diseases and then contacts you to make arrangements for a more complete diagnosis and/or treatment.
c. Pediatrician or Physician — Diagnoses and treats childhood diseases and accidents. Refers to specialists if necessary.
d. The Allergy Foundation of America, 801 Second Ave., New York, New York 10017 — Provides publications related to allergic diseases.
e. The American Diabetes Association, Inc., 18 E. 48th Street, New York, New York 10017 — Provides cookbooks, names of camps for diabetic children, and a bimonthly magazine concerning diabetes.
f. Epilepsy Foundation of America, 733 15th Street N.W., Washington, D.C. 20005 — Provides free literature concerning the problems and needs of epilepsy.

g. National Tuberculosis and Respiratory Diseases Association, 1740 Broadway, New York, New York 10019 — Provides books and pamphlets concerning respiratory diseases and aids local chapters in helping parents and teachers develop child-health programs. Canada also has a similar organization called the Canadian Tuberculosis and Respiratory Disease Association, 343 O'Connor Street, Ottawa 4, Ontario.

h. American Academy of Pediatrics, 1801 Hinman Ave., Evanston, Illinois 60204 — Provides information to parents on child-health problems.

Have Pals for Auditory Problems

a. Classroom Teachers — Observe symptoms of auditory problems and refer to school nurse for further screening.

b. School Nurse — Screens by giving the child a hearing test and then informs you of the results. The school nurse may suggest that you take the child to a hearing specialist.

c. Speech-Hearing Therapist — Can also diagnose auditory problems and provide instruction to help the child learn.

d. Otologist — A medical specialist who deals with the ear and its diseases. An otologist can diagnose and treat your child's ears.

e. Otolaryngologist — A medical specialist who treats ear, nose, and throat problems.

f. Alexander Graham Bell Association for the Deaf, Inc., 1537 35th Street N.W., Washington, D.C. 20007 — Helps parents understand the special problems of deaf children and provides free information kits on speech, hearing, and education of deaf children. A similar association in Canada is the Canadian Association of the Deaf, 56A Wellesley Street East, Toronto, Ontario.

Have Pals for Visual Problems

a. The Classroom Teacher — Observes symptoms of visual problems and refers to school nurse.

b. School Nurse — Screens child for possible visual problems and makes recommendations to parents.

c. Ophthalmologist or Oculist — A medical specialist concerned with the eye and diseases of the eye.

d. Optometrist — A non-medical specialist who measures and corrects vision and provides visual training activities.

e. Optician — Craftsman skilled in grinding lenses and the making and fitting of glasses.

f. National Society for the Prevention of Blindness, 79 Madison Avenue, New York, New York 10016 — Offers publications concerning the prevention of blindness and eye health and safety. The Pointing E Test which was recommended in Chapter Two is one of the publications available from this agency. A similar agency in Canada is The Canadian National Institute for the Blind, 1929 Bayview Avenue, Toronto, Ontario M4G 3E8.

Have Pals for Educational Problems

a. The Classroom Teacher — The teacher has the major responsibility for providing meaningful, relevant, and interesting instruction for your child and also for informing you of your child's progress.

b. Principal — The principal is the instructional leader in the school. He has the responsibility of helping the teachers provide an excellent educational program. In addition, he arranges the special programs and services which the school offers.

c. Remedial Reading Teacher — Provides remedial reading instruction to those children who need it most and are expected to profit most from this intensive and systematic instruction.

d. Reading Resource Teachers — Reading specialists who help classroom teachers by providing suggestions for organizing the reading program, selecting appropriate materials, and suggesting valuable methods and techniques.

e. Visiting Teacher — Member of the school staff who works with children and their families when the child is experiencing difficulty. The visiting teacher helps integrate the school and community services for the benefit of the child. Often visiting teachers can tell you of local agencies and sources of help for your child's particular problem.

f. Special Education Teachers — Many schools have special education programs for children who are mentally retarded, deaf, learning disabled, gifted, physically handicapped, and so forth. These teachers have been trained in the special techniques which are necessary for adapting the instruction to the capabilities and limitations of children with varying exceptionalities.

g. Private Remedial Reading Clinics and Tutors — Diagnose the reading difficulties of children and plan programs for correcting them using activities and methods which seem most appropriate for the child.

h. Day Care and Child Development Council of America, 1426 H Street N.W., Washington D.C. 20005 — This organization provides information concerning organizing day care centers, and offers many publications concerning programs for young children.

Have Pals for Parental Causes

a. Friends — People need people. Talk with your friends who have children to get ideas on ways they handle their children. Also read some of the popular magazines which include descriptions of how parents handle certain problems. The magazine which I recommend most highly for parents is *Parents' Magazine*. The address for subscriptions is 80 Newbridge Road, Bergenfield, New Jersey 07621.

b. Books — Refer to Appendix I for suggested books. Most of these are available at your local bookstore.

c. Committee on Parenthood Education — This is a relatively new organization which is trying to establish local agencies throughout

145

the country. The organization publishes a newsletter which you can receive by writing to Cope, PO Box 9533, San Diego, Calif.

d. United States Department of Health, Education and Welfare, Office of Child Development, Washington, D.C. 20201 — Many government publications are available to assist parents in rearing their children. Write for a current list of publications. A similar organization in Canada is the Canadian Home and School and Parent-Teacher Federation, 240 Eglinton Ave. E., Toronto, Ontario, and the Department of National Health and Welfare, Child and Adult Health Services, Brooke Claxton Building, Tunney's Pasture, Ottawa, Ontario. In addition to providing educational material for parents, the latter organization publishes a handbook, entitled *The Canadian Mother and Child*.

e. Parent-Teacher Association — Your local chapter of the Parent-Teacher Association probably offers many programs which help you understand the new programs in schools, as well as learning more about dealing with your child.

Have Pals for Aptitudinal Problems

a. The Classroom Teacher — Observes behavior and is a specialist in determining the achievement levels of your child and is responsible for planning programs based on his needs.

b. School Psychologist — Provides intensive and individual studies of students resulting in information and understanding which are shared with the teachers and you. Most school psychologists will make recommendations for ways of dealing with your child and/or other follow-up services which are necessary.

c. Child Study Clinics — A support facility to service children who are experiencing difficulty with school work. Generally, an interdisciplinary staff made up of educators, pediatricians, and psychologists works together to diagnose and counsel problems related to adjusting to school, learning disabilities, aptitudes, and behavior problems.

d. The National Association for Gifted Children, 8080 Spring Valley Drive, Cincinnati, Ohio 45236 — Provides consulting services for children, adults, agencies, and others to encourage support and understanding of courses for gifted children.

e. The Association for Children with Learning Disabilities, 2200 Brownsville Road, Pittsburgh, Penna. 15210 — Provides information for parents and professionals concerning camps, schools, and publications which enable people to understand children who have adequate intelligence, but experience difficulty learning. Contact your local agency for special lectures, publications, and information or services.

f. National Association for Retarded Children, 2709 Avenue E, East Arlington, Texas 76011 — Provides information to improve the education of retarded children. A similar organization in Canada is the Canadian Association for the Mentally Retarded, Kinsmen NIMR

Building, York University, 4700 Keele Street, Downsview, Ontario. This sponsors many local associations which assist parents in selecting schools, summer camps, and suggestions for working with the mentally retarded.

g. Neurologist — A medical specialist who evaluates the development and functioning of the central nervous system.

h. School Guidance Counselor — One who helps the students make adjustments and choices especially related to vocations, education, and personal matters. Guidance counselors help children find their special aptitudes.

Have Pals for Language Problems

a. The Classroom Teacher — Observes the child and may refer to the speech and hearing therapist.

b. Speech and Hearing Therapist — Works individually or with small groups of children to help them develop particular sounds and/or language patterns.

c. Language Pathologist — Studies disorders of the entire spectrum of communication and verbal behavior by analyzing normal language development.

d. Speech Pathologist — Studies the abnormalities of articulation and provides suggestions for correcting speech problems.

e. Many of the agencies which were mentioned above also can be of value in helping children with language problems. For example, the Association for Children with Learning Disabilities, the agencies for the deaf, neurologists, and hearing specialists work together to help children who are experiencing language problems.

Have Pals for Social-Emotional Problems

a. The Classroom Teacher — Observes problems and symptoms.

b. Guidance Counselors — Help children express and deal with their feelings and problems.

c. Visiting Teacher — Works closely with the home and other community agencies to help children overcome social-emotional problems.

d. Clergy — Offer counseling services for children and parents.

e. School Psychologist — Diagnoses and makes recommendations based on problems children might be experiencing.

f. Clinical Psychologists — A specialist with a Ph.D. degree in clinical psychology who studies persons suffering from emotional disorders.

g. Psychiatrist — A physician whose specialty is the diagnosis and treatment of mental disorders.

h. Psychometrist — One who administers, scores, and interprets psychological tests. A psychometrist shares the test results with other specialists in the schools, such as the school psychologist, or school psychiatrist who make recommendations based on the results of the test.

147

i. Psychiatric Social Worker — A person specially trained in analyzing and interpreting the social conditions in the home, school, and neighborhood.

j. The American Association of Psychiatric Services for Children, 250 W. 57th Street, New York, New York 10019 — An association which helps parents select an appropriate clinic in the local community.

k. The Child Study Association of America, 9 East 89th Street, New York, New York, 10028 — Emphasizes the importance of family mental health and offers a wide range of programs designed to help improve family life with special emphasis on the role of the parent.

l. The National Association of Mental Health, Inc., 10 Columbus Circle, New York, New York 10019 — Provides pamphlets and other information services for parents of mentally ill children. Check your telephone directory for a local chapter since many of them provide parent education programs. A similar organization in Canada is The Canadian Mental Health Association, 2160 Yonge Street, Suite 304, Toronto M4S 2Z3.

m. Big Brothers of America, 341 Suburban Station Building, Philadelphia, Pennsylvania 19103 — This organization is designed to help boys between the ages of eight and eighteen who do not have fathers. If you believe that your child is experiencing some social-emotional problems due to lack of a male figure, you may want to write this organization for more information.

n. Books for Children — There are many books for children to help face problems. Ask your librarian what books she recommends concerning bossiness, changes and new places, death, discontent, disobedience, family life, fears, friendships, frustrations, physical handicaps, getting along with and understanding others, hurt feelings, loneliness, manners, responsibilities, and temper.

Your Role in Helping Your Child

Isn't it nice to know that you have so many pals? Keep in mind that this is a sample list of the help which is available. Your child's teacher, principal, school psychologist, pediatrician, and other pals can suggest even more specialists. In addition, they will be able to give you information concerning local specialists which they recommend highly and/or local chapters of some of the national agencies which were mentioned above. Take advantage of all the help available.

You will probably first become aware of your child's problems in learning to read from seeing his daily papers, report cards, or when talking with his teacher. Or, you may suspect he is not progressing as well as possible when he experiences the same difficulties time and time again. Your first step is to call the teacher for an appointment to discuss your child's reading and his behavior in school. Of course if your child is a preschooler, you should make an appointment to discuss him with your pediatrician. If the teacher, school psychologist, pediatrician, or others determine that your child is experiencing difficulties due to some of the factors which influence achievement in reading and other academic areas, they will guide you to the right pals.

Remedial instruction may be suggested for your child. If the school does not offer such instruction, or, if you prefer, you may take your child to a private reading clinic or employ a tutor for remedial reading work. The following guidelines should be kept in mind when selecting a reading clinic or tutor:

1. A diagnosis is made to determine the child's reading levels, specific skill needs, interests, and special aptitudes.

2. Instruction is provided during the time of day when the child is most attentive. This may mean that you will have to get special permission to take the child out of school for an hour and then take him back.

3. A variety of materials and methods which are new to the child are used, rather than the same methods that have already failed.

4. The areas in which the clinician and child work are free from distractions.

5. Specific goals are established after diagnosing the child's needs. A conference is scheduled to inform you of the results of the diagnosis, specific plans for instruction, and a tour of the facilities.

6. Conferences are scheduled frequently to keep you aware of the progress your child is making to provide you with specific recommendations about what you can do to help. Conferences are held with the child's teacher to determine what the child is doing in school and to relate the remedial program in which your child is involved.

7. The teachers and clinicians have a strong background in reading and experiences in working successfully with children.

Be leery of reading clinics which promise instant success with some new method or technique. Also, determine if the clinic is honest when considering clients, taking only those who will profit from their services. Be suspicious of those clinics which place emphasis on expensive machines which may be motivational, but do not significantly increase reading achievement.

Your cooperation with the tutor or clinic is extremely important. Make sure you have frequent conferences to determine what you can do to help. Show the clinician or tutor this book and ask him what games, ideas, and activities you should be using.

Your reaction to your child's reading problem is very important. Your love and acceptance are needed more than ever. Be honest with him concerning the fact that he is experiencing difficulty, but at the same time provide that ray of hope that he can do better. Help him realize his strengths. Point out that all children are different — they vary in height, weight, interest, *and* reading achievement.

You are a VIP. You help your child *v*alue reading, you show *i*nterest in his reading achievement, and you *p*rovide basic necessities and specialized help if necessary. Have pals, have patience, and have pleasant times as you help your child learn to read.

APPENDIX A

TESTING YOUR CHILD'S KNOWLEDGE OF PHONICS

The following tests can be used to determine what to teach your child. You will notice that some of the words on the tests are nonsense syllables. Nonsense syllables are used so the child must sound out the word rather than pronounce it by sight.

Test for Visual Discrimination of Letters — Kindergarten Level

Directions: Ask the child to point to the letter that *is not like the others.* If the child misses more than one item, try the activities for visual skills in Chapter 2.

1.	o	o	x	o	6.	M	M	N	M
2.	a	b	a	a	7.	G	G	J	G
3.	c	c	d	c	8.	H	H	B	H
4.	b	d	b	b	9.	E	E	E	O
5.	p	b	b	b	10.	W	W	V	W

Test for Visual Discrimination of Words — Kindergarten Level

Directions: Ask the child to point to the word that *is not like the other ones in the row.* Do not expect the child to read the words. If your child misses more than one of the items, try the activities for visual skills in Chapter 2.

1.	win	win	window	win
2.	have	have	have	had
3.	see	seen	see	see
4.	bed	bad	bed	bed
5.	it	it	at	it
6.	and	end	and	and
7.	come	came	come	come
8.	dad	dad	dad	bad
9.	bake	bake	bike	bake
10.	was	saw	was	was

Test for Auditory Discrimination — Kindergarten Level

Directions: Read each row of words twice and ask the child to tell you the word that *does not rhyme.* If the child misses more than one, try the activities for auditory skills in Chapter 2.

1.	book	look	face
2.	make	took	take

3.	sit	hit	mat
4.	hat	hen	bat
5.	kite	fight	fit
6.	rang	sing	bang
7.	wet	bat	sat
8.	see	bee	been
9.	they	then	say
10.	when	band	sand

Test for Auditory Discrimination of Beginning Sounds — Kindergarten Level

Directions: Pronounce the three words in each row. Ask the child to tell you which one *begins* with a different sound. If the child misses more than one, use the activities for auditory skills in Chapter 2.

1.	cat	come	do
2.	wind	been	won
3.	jam	back	beak
4.	do	did	bid
5.	go	to	tow
6.	be	pet	bet
7.	happy	have	fight
8.	set	so	rat
9.	get	jet	go
10.	cake	cent	coke

Test for Auditory Discrimination — Kindergarten Level

Directions: Say the following pairs of words and ask your child to tell you if the words are the *same* or *different*. If the child misses more than one, use the activities for auditory skills in Chapter 2.

1.	wet	—	bet
2.	do	—	do
3.	say	—	pay
4.	now	—	new
5.	set	—	sit
6.	can	—	can
7.	bat	—	bit
8.	mat	—	nat
9.	cat	—	cat
10.	bad	—	dad

Test of Letter Knowledge

Directions: Ask the child to *read the names of the letters to you*. If the child misses any, use the suggested activities on letter names in Chapter 2.

o	z	v	d	b
q	f	x	s	h
y	g	e	j	p
u	w	c	a	l
m	i	k	n	t
		r		

Test for Initial Consonants — First Grade Level

Directions: Ask the child to say the nonsense words listed below. Listen to see if the *first sound is pronounced correctly*. If the child misses any, use the suggested activities for consonant sounds in Chapter 3.

bad	jad	rad
cad	kad	sad
dad	lad	tad
fad	mad	vad
gad	nad	wad
had	pad	yad

Test for Final Consonant Sounds — First-Second Grade Levels

Directions: Ask the child to pronounce the following nonsense words. Notice if he *pronounces the final sound correctly*. If the child misses any of them, use the suggested activities on consonant sounds in Chapter 3.

mab	maj	man
mad	mak	map
maf	mal	mas
mag	mam	mat

Test for Common Sound Patterns — First Grade Level

Directions: Ask your child to pronounce these *common sound patterns*. If the child misses any, use the suggested activities on sound patterns in Chapter 3.

all	an
at	ill
it	ell
et	ay
en	ake
in	or

Test for Consonant Combinations — First Grade and Second Grade Levels

Directions: Ask the child to pronounce the following nonsense words. Listen to see if the *consonant combinations* are pronounced correctly. If the child misses any, use the suggested activities on consonant sounds in Chapter 3.

shan	fran	flan
stan	whan	clan
blan	than	glan
plan	chan	span
tran	sman	snan
chan	twan	

Test for Sight Vocabulary — First-Second Grade Levels

Directions: Ask the child to *read each of the following words within three seconds*. Expose one word at a time. If the child misses any, use the suggested activities for sight words in Chapter 4.

1. are	10. her	19. of	28. with
2. come	11. look	20. or	29. did
3. he	12. on	21. soon	30. in
4. it	13. saw	22. them	31. their
5. out	14. bring	23. about	32. then
6. run	15. was	24. good	33. use
7. you	16. but	25. me	34. very
8. by	17. give	26. that	35. went
9. for	18. had	27. they	36. which

Test for Short Vowel Sounds — Second Grade Level

Directions: Ask the child to pronounce each of the following words. Notice if he says the correct short vowel sound. If the child misses any, use the suggested activities for vowel sounds in Chapter 3.

1. bag	3. big	5. bug	7. peg	9. pog
2. beg	4. bog	6. pag	8. pig	10. pug

Test for the Sounds of C — Second Grade Level

Directions: Ask the child to pronounce the following "words." See if he knows the c followed by i, e, or y, usually makes the s sound. When c is followed by a, o, or u, it usually makes the k sound. If the child misses any of the words, use the suggested activities on consonant sounds in Chapter 3.

1.	cap	6.	cof
2.	cip	7.	cil
3.	cep	8.	ces
4.	cop	9.	cam
5.	cup	10.	cus

Test for the Sounds of G — Second Grade Level

Directions: Ask the child to pronounce the following "words." See if he knows that g followed by i, e, or y, usually makes the j sound. G followed by a, o, and u, usually makes the g sound. If the child misses any of the words, use the suggested activities on consonant sounds in Chapter 3.

1.	gam	6.	gad
2.	gen	7.	ged
3.	git	8.	gid
4.	gyp	9.	got
5.	gup	10.	gud

Test for Long Vowel Sounds and Open Syllables — Second Grade Level

Directions: Ask the child to pronounce the following "words." See if he says the *long vowel sound*. If the child misses any, use the suggested activities on vowel sounds in Chapter 3.

1.	ba	6.	ka
2.	be	7.	ke
3.	bi	8.	ki
4.	bo	9.	ko
5.	bu	10.	ku

Test for Closed Syllables — Second Grade Level

Directions: Ask the child to pronounce the following "words." See if he pronounces the *short vowel sound*. If he misses any, use the suggested activities on vowel sounds in Chapter 3.

1.	peb	6.	heb
2.	pib	7.	hib
3.	pob	8.	hub
4.	pub	9.	hab
5.	pab	10.	hob

Test for Final E Principle — Second Grade Level

Directions: Ask the child to pronounce the following "words." Listen to see if he pronounces the first vowel long. He should not pronounce the final e because it is silent.

1.	nobe	6.	tobe
2.	nibe	7.	tube
3.	nube	8.	tibe
4.	nebe	9.	tebe
5.	nabe	10.	tabe

Test for the Bossy R — Second Grade Level

Directions: Ask the child to pronounce the following "words." See if he says the vowel sound influenced by "r." If the child misses any, use the suggested activities on vowel sounds in Chapter 3.

1.	der	8.	mer
2.	dir	9.	mir
3.	dur	10.	mur
4.	dor	11.	mor
5.	dar	12.	mar
6.	dare	13.	mare
7.	dere	14.	mere

Test for Diphthongs — Second Grade Level

Directions: Ask the child to pronounce the following "words." Notice if he says the correct sound — oi as in oil or ou as in ouch or cow. If he misses any, use the suggested activities on vowel sounds in Chapter 3.

1.	boil	6.	loy
2.	noil	7.	out
3.	foy	8.	oud
4.	pow	9.	poil
5.	boy	10.	pout

Test for Syllabication 1 — Third Grade Level

Directions: Ask the child to pronounce these nonsense words. As he pronounces them, notice if he has divided the words into syllables between the double consonants. You can also listen to see if he pronounces the short vowel sounds in the final syllable (closed syllable). If he misses any, use the suggested activities for dividing words into syllables in Chapter 3.

1.	dabber	6.	fobter
2.	remter	7.	pattor
3.	sommer	8.	labber
4.	hoppin	9.	comter
5.	ribbet	10.	hallow

Test for Syllabication 2 — Third Grade Level

Directions: Ask the child to pronounce the following nonsense words. See if he divides the words into syllables after the first vowel. You can also listen to hear if he pronounces the long vowel sound in the first syllable (open syllable). If he misses any, use the suggested activities for dividing words into syllables in Chapter 3.

1. doter
2. hoger
3. sadet
4. tapid
5. fobis
6. baple
7. higer
8. judis
9. potel
10. setin

Test for Syllabication 3 — Third Grade Level

Directions: Ask the child to pronounce the following nonsense words. See if he includes the consonant preceding le with the le to form the last syllable. If he misses any, use the suggested activities for dividing words into syllables in Chapter 3.

1. fakle
2. pokle
3. bidle
4. hekle
5. fumble
6. burple
7. herkle
8. rample
9. tible
10. gable

Test for Prefixes and Suffixes — Third Grade Level

Directions: Ask the child to read the following "words." See if he notices the prefix or suffix and pronounces it as a separate syllable. If he misses any, use the suggested activities for structural analysis in Chapter 4.

1. balling
2. reban
3. ungate
4. cupable
5. inpay
6. presoon
7. rugly
8. excry
9. deskous
10. pailful

APPENDIX B

MAKING HARD-COVER BOOKS

Suggestions by Janice Gross

Materials

1. Rubber cement
2. Scissors
3. Book stapler or sewing machine
4. Precut 8″ x 14″ blank paper
5. 8″ x 14″ construction paper
6. 9″ x 15″ piece of thin cardboard
7. 11″ x 16″ piece of fabric

(1) Gather materials

(2) Lay 9″ x 15″ card-
board flat on table

(3) Place 1 piece of
8″ x 14″ construction
paper centered on
cardboard

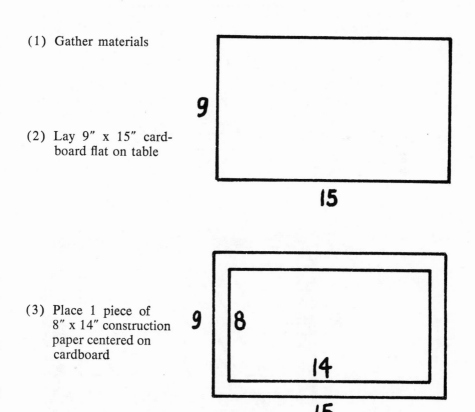

(4) Place desired amount of 8″ x 14″ blank pages on top of construction paper

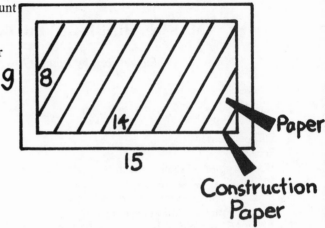

(5) Staple or sew your assemblage down the center

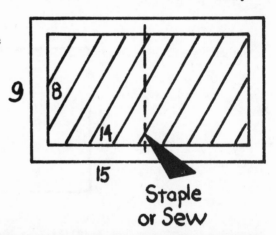

(6) Place sewn assemblage centered on top of piece of material

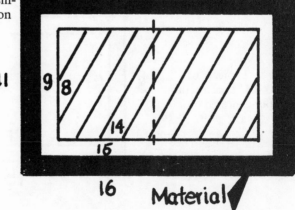

(7) Fold construction paper and blank pages in half. Lift both halves to expose cardboard lying flat on material. A slit in the material should be cut in the center on the 2 "length sides"

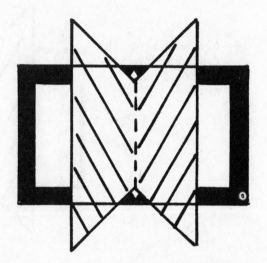

(8) Put rubber cement on corners and sides of material and edges of cardboard. Fold in edges of material snuggly around edge of cardboard. Be careful not to pull too tight

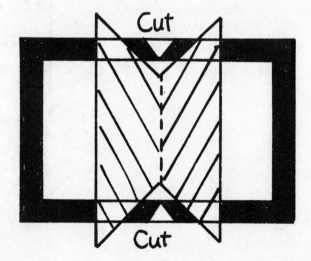

(9) Cement construction
paper down over
cardboard and
material

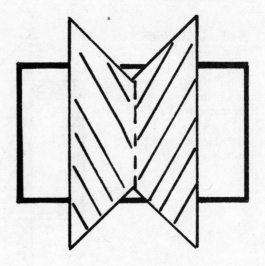

(10) Fold book (card-
board, material, and
all) in half. You now
have your own hard-
cover book.

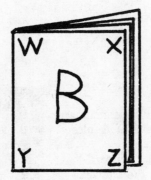

APPENDIX C

SAMPLE RECORDS FOR CHILDREN

It is not possible to list all available records which have companion books. The following list will give you a sample of a few favorite recordings/books.

Kimbo Educational, Box 246, Deal, New Jersey, offers the following records with companion books. Write for a complete catalogue.

Aesop's Fables
Pinocchio
Peter and the Wolf
The Wizard of Oz
Cinderella
Oliver Twist

Kimbo Educational also offers the Ready—Set—Read-Along Series. It is a self-directing, learning series that introduces alphabet letters, shapes, numbers by means of cartoons, silly selections, puzzles, stories, and games.

Book 1 — *Do You See Sillies?*
Book 2 — *Do You See Shapes?*
Book 3 — *Do You See Numbers and Numerals?*

The Scholastic Record and Book Companion Series includes records and paperback books at reasonable prices. Over forty titles, including the following, are available from Scholastic Audio-Visual, 906 Sylvan Ave., Englewood Cliffs, New Jersey 07632.

The Biggest Bear
Clifford Gets a Job
Caps for Sale
Curious George Rides a Bike
Jack and the Beanstalk
Old MacDonald Had a Farm

The Walt Disney Companion Series is a collection of eight records and books including:

Sleeping Beauty
Winnie the Pooh
101 Dalmatians
Mother Goose Rhymes
Peter and the Wolf
Three Little Pigs
Dumbo
Bedknobs and Broomsticks

These are available in department stores, or from Walt Disney Music Company, 175 Community Drive, Great Neck, New York 11021

APPENDIX D

SELECTED PERIODICALS FOR CHILDREN

Listed below are selected periodicals for children. For more information and titles, refer to *The Dobler World Dictionary of Youth Periodicals: Third Edition*. This reference book gives current data on nearly 1,000 magazines and newspapers prepared specifically for young people both here and abroad. Ask your local librarian if she has this resource.

American Girl. Girl Scouts of the U.S.A., 830 Third Ave., New York, New York, 10022, (8 years and up).

Boy's Life. Boy Scouts of America, New Brunswick, New Jersey, 08903 (8 years and up).

Calling All Girls. Better Reading Foundation, Inc., 52 Vanderbilt Ave., New York, New York, 10017, (Ages 7-14).

Child Life. Child Life, Inc., 817 W. Market St., Louisville, Kentucky, 40202, (5-10 years).

Children's Digest. Parents' Magazine Enterprises, Inc., Bergenfield, New Jersey, 07612, (6-12 years).

Children's Playcraft. Parents' Magazine Enterprises, Inc., Bergenfield, New Jersey, 07612.

Children's Playmate. Children's Playmate Magazine, Inc., 629 Union Ave., Cleveland, Ohio, 44105, (6-12 years).

Ebony Jr! Johnson Publishing Co., 820 South Michigan Ave., Chicago, Ill., 60605.

Electric Company Magazine. North Road, Poughkeepsie, New York, 12601, (3-8 years).

Highlights for Children. Highlights for Children, 2300 W. 5th Avenue, Columbus, Ohio, 43200, (6-12 years).

Humpty Dumpty's Magazine for Little Children. Parents' Magazine Enterprises, Inc., Bergenfield, New Jersey, 07612, (3-7 years.).

Jack and Jill. Curtiss Publishing Company, Independence Square, Philadelphia, Pennsylvania, 19100, (4-10 years).

Kids. Kid's Publishers, Inc., 777 Third Avenue, New York, New York, 10017.

Mechanics Illustrated. Fawcett Publishers, Inc., Fawcett Place, Greenwich, Conn., 06830.

Model Airplane News. Air Age Inc., 551 Fifth Ave., New York, New York, 10036, (Ages 8 and up).

My Weekly Reader. American Education Publications, Xerox Education Center, Columbus, Ohio, 43216. Separate issues for kindergarten through sixth grade.

Nature and Science. Natural History Press, Garden City, New York, 11530, (Ages 8 and up).

Pack-O-Fun. Clapper Publishing Company, Inc., P.O. Box 568, Park Ridge, Ill., 60068, (Ages 6-12).

Popular Science Monthly. Popular Science Publishing, Inc., 355 Lexington Ave., New York, New York, 10017 (4-12 grades).

Scholastic News Pilot, News Ranger, New Trails, New Explorer and News Time. Scholastic Magazines and Book Service, 50 W. 44th Street, New York, New York, 10036.

Sesame Street Magazine. North Road, Poughkeepsie, New York, 12601, (3-7 years).

Wee Wisdom. Unity School of Christianity, Lee's Summit, Missouri, 64063, (6-11 years).

World Traveler. Published by the Alexander Graham Bell Association for the Deaf, Inc., 1537 35th Street, N.W., Washington, D.C., 20007.

APPENDIX E

SELECTED COMMERCIAL READING GAMES
AND ACTIVITIES

Hundreds of games and activity books are available to help children develop particular reading skills. Many of these are available at local department stores. If not, you may want to write for a catalogue.

Educational Cards, Inc., 1302 Industrial Bank Bldg., Detroit, Michigan, offers the following:

> Edu-Cards Puzzle Lottos — On the Farm
>> Around the House
>
> ABC Lotto
> Zoo Lotto
> Farm Lotto
> Go-Together Lotto
> Object Lotto
> The World About Us Lotto
> Canned Alphabet
> Letter Recognition Game

Garrard Publishing Company, Champaign, Illinois 61820, offers the following:

> Dolch Popper words — Sets One and Two.
>> Set One includes the easiest 110 words.
>> Set Two contains the more difficult 110 basic sight words.
>
> Sight Phrase Cards by Dolch
> The Syllable Game by Dolch
> My Puzzle Book One and Two
> Picture Readiness Game — one or more can play
> Who Gets It? — Dolch Reading Readiness Game
> Match Game. Sets One and Two.
>> A picture-word match game for teaching the 95 most common nouns.

Ideal School Supply Company, 11000 S. Lavergne Ave., Oak Lawn, Ill. 60453, offers the following:

> End-In-E-Game — Silent E
> Space Flight Game — Blends, Vocabulary
> Rhyming Zig Zag
> Sea of Vowels — Long and Short Vowel Sounds
> Silly Sounds — Consonants

Kenworthy Educational Services, Inc., P.O. Box 3031, Buffalo, New York 14205, offers the following:

Word Builders
ABC Game
Word and Phrase Sentence Builder
Rainbow Word Builders
Syllable Flip Cards
Word Blends
Word Prefixes
Word Suffixes
Word Family Fun
Picture-Phonic Cards
Dog House Game
Say The Sounds
Junior Phonic Rummy
Phonic Rummy
Phonetic Word Drill Cards
Your Child Can Learn To Read
I Learn To Read (Books 1 and 2)

Milton-Bradley, Springfield, Mass., 01101, offers the following:

Picture Card Games — Sets I and II
Scene Sequence Cards
Animal Puzzles
Wood Board Match Ups
Consonant Wheels
Vowel Wheels
You Can Read Phonetic Drill Cards
Educational Password
Sort-A-Card Readiness Game
Pairs Word Game
Pick-Pairs Game

Additional Recommended Resources

Bowmar Publishing Company, Glendale, California 91201 offers:

Gold Cup Games (Grades 3-12)
Dune Buggy Rally
Horse Trail Ride
Motorcycle Moto Cross

Western Publishing Company, Inc., Racine, Wisconsin offers:

Golden Readiness Workbooks

My Weekly Reader, Xerox Education Center, Columbus, Ohio 43216 offers:

My Weekly Reader Practice Books
First Step in Reading
Surprise Yourself (Perception puzzles for kindergarten)
Phonics and Word Power
Introducing Table and Graph Skills
Listening Skills

Modern Curriculum Press, 13900 Prospect Road, Cleveland, Ohio 44136 offers:

Phonics Is Fun — Books 1, 2, 3
Phonics Workbook — Books A, B, C

APPENDIX F

WORDS AND GENERALIZATIONS CONCERNING PHONICS

Consonant Sounds

Listed below are simple words for each of the 24 consonant sounds which were listed in Chapter Three.

b	*ch*	*d*	*f*
baby	chair	dog	fat
ball	chore	door	for
banana	cherries	day	feed
bath	chill	dinner	fit
belt	child	dish	five
bike	cheese	dollar	fast
book	chocolate	down	fall
bomb	chief	dad	few
boat	chat	did	foot
by	chart	duck	fair

g	*h*	*j*	*k*
got	happy	job	cook
goat	how	giraffe	key
get	hot	jacks	cat
give	help	jet	kid
gave	hold	joke	kitchen
gas	hand	jump	kitten
gold	had	just	come
go	hit	joy	call
goose	hat	jingle	carry
gun	hard	gentle	color

l	*m*	*n*	*ng*
little	man	no	sing
like	make	never	finger
lie	mother	name	rang
lay	meet	not	thing
lady	made	need	hung
less	money	new	bang
land	my	night	ping-pong
library	move	note	hang
line	meal	nut	sang
listen	monster	now	ding-dong

p	*r*	*s*	*sh*
pay	rat	see	shell
paper	race	saw	shake
paint	run	seven	shoot
pack	rake	save	shoe
pet	red	sorry	shirt
peach	rest	some	she
pepper	row	said	shut
pie	rose	say	ship
pig	rag	sat	sharp
poor	rub	sit	sheep

t	*th* (voiceless)	*th* (voiced)	*v*
take	thin	then	vase
tie	third	there	violin
took	thing	they	vowed
time	thumb	that	vein
ten	thaw	this	velvet
table	thick	the	vent
tea	thought	than	vest
tear	thousand	their	vine
touch	thermometer	them	visitor
today	thank	though	very

w	*wh*	*y*	*z*
wash	what	yard	zap
waste	wheel	yellow	zebra
wait	when	year	zero
water	where	yell	zig-zag
we	which	yes	zip
went	why	yet	zipper
want	white	young	zone
way	whistle	your	zoo
week	whisper	yoyo	zoom
well	while	yoke	zinc

166

Consonant Blends

bl	*br*	*cl*
black	brace	class
blade	brain	clay
blanket	branch	clean
blue	bread	clear
blind	break	clerk
blister	brick	climb
block	bridge	clock
blond	broom	close
bloom	brown	clothes
blow	brush	club

cr	*dr*	*fl*
crack	drag	flag
cradle	drank	flat
crash	drapery	flavor
cream	draw	flea
crib	dream	flight
crime	drew	float
crocodile	drill	flood
cross	drive	floor
crow	drop	flower
cry	dry	fly

fr	*gl*	*gr*
frame	glad	grade
free	glass	grain
freeze	glove	grand
fresh	gland	gravy
Friday	globe	gray
fright	glee	green
frog	glen	great
from	glare	gross
front	glance	ground
fry	glider	grease

pl	*pr*	*sc, sch, sk*
plane	pretzel	scale
plant	price	skirt
plan	princess	scout
place	print	school
plastic	prize	scooter
play	program	scarf
please	promise	score
plug	provide	skip
plumber	principal	skate
plus	proud	sky

sl	*sm*	*sn*
slam	smack	snap
slap	small	snip
slave	smart	sneeze
sleep	smash	snore
slice	smell	snake
slide	smile	snail
slim	smoke	sniff
slow	smooth	sniffle
slug	smudge	sneak
slip	smother	snow

sp	*st*	*tr*
space	stew	track
spark	step	trade
special	start	trail
speed	stand	train
spell	state	travel
spice	sting	tray
spin	still	treat
spoon	stone	tree
spot	stood	tried
spy	stop	trip

Consonant Generalizations or Rules

In addition to learning the consonant sounds, there are some generalizations concerning consonant sounds children should learn. The most frequently used rules for consonant sounds are:

a. Only the second consonant is heard in words like *g*nat, *w*rite, *k*nee and wa*l*k. In other words, sometimes a consonant is silent.

b. When two alike consonants appear together, the first one is sounded and the second one is silent. (sit ing, háp é)

c. The first consonant is heard in words like la*mb*, *sc*ent, *sw*ord, o*ft*en, and *gh*ost. Again some consonants do not make a sound in the word.

d. The /f/ sound can be represented by ph as in photo; the /sh/ sound by /ch/ as in machine.

e. Qu has the /kw/ sound as in queen, or the /k/ sound as in conquer.

f. The letter s represents different sounds: /s/ as in sell, /z/ as in his, and /sh/ as in sugar.

g. The consonants c and g have two sounds:
   —Usually c is /k/ in words like care, coke, cube, and other words when c is followed by a, o, and u.
   —Usually g is /j/ in gem, giant, gypsy, and other words when c is followed by e, i, and y.
   —Usually g is /j/ in gem, gypsy, and other words when c is followed by e, i, and y.
   —Usually g is /g/ in go, game, gum, and other words when g is followed by a, o, and u.

h. The letter x represents three different sounds: /x/ as in xylem and Xerox, /ks/ as in six or box, and /gz/ as in example and exit.

Vowel Sounds

Listed below are sample words for each of the vowel sounds listed in Chapter Three.

short a	short e	short i	short o	short u
fat	bed	Indian	stop	up
mad	beg	fit	hot	us
add	egg	kid	pop	sun
fast	wet	pick	not	cut
black	west	is	on	rug
glad	end	in	off	bud
apple	step	his	October	much
back	chest	it	ox	tub
last	peg	sit	pot	pup
tan	set	mix	pod	but

long a	long e	long i	long o	long u
say	eat	like	open	cute
pay	feed	I	over	use
may	bee	bike	boat	new
rain	tree	by	soap	cue
ape	mean	mice	snow	blue
ate	east	die	row	rude
way	team	ride	coat	unit
pain	see	pipe	home	few
take	seat	nice	rope	duke
day	beads	pie	goat	yule

a as in air	a as in car	e as in hear, irrigate
air	bar	dear
fair	car	fear
bear	are	gear
carry	hard	irrigate
hair	farm	irresponsible
fare	tar	near
marry	scar	deer
tear	far	peer
pear	guard	queer
pair	heart	year

er as in her, first, burn	or as in horn	long oo as in tool
earth	orange	zoo
heard	for	too
dirt	war	food
fir	organ	choose
her	more	spoon
burn	poor	balloon
sir	sore	pool
jury	score	goose
higher	tore	soon
hurt	door	room

short oo as in book	oi, oy as in toy	ow, ou as in cow
cook	boy	cow
foot	toy	ouch
stood	oil	couch
brook	boil	pound
hook	point	our
rookie	joy	count
took	moist	house
look	poison	how
stood	soil	now
nook	spoil	town

Vowel Rules and Generalizations

Since there are so many vowel sounds, children must learn the generalizations or rules which help them to know what sound the vowels have in different words. The following vowel rules are the ones that are the most frequently applied.

a. When a one-syllable word or accented syllable contains two vowels, one of which is a final *e,* the first vowel usually represents its long sound and the final *e* is silent.

rake	bike	bake	cake
bone	ate	lake	game
ride	race	use	place

b. When a word or syllable ends in a vowel (open syllable), the vowel sound is usually long.

he	go	be	vacation
by	she	we	fly
table	open	why	

c. When a word or syllable ends in a consonant (closed syllable), the vowel sound is usually short.

bad	hid	fan	can
sit	fat	in	sing
bet	sun	hot	on

d. When *i* is followed by *gh, nd,* or *ld,* as in find, child, and light, the *i* usually represents its long sound. The vowel o followed by ld usually has a long sound as in old.

e. If the only vowel in a word or syllable is an *a* followed by w, ll, and u, the sound of the a is usually short o as in "tall."

f. When two vowel letters appear together in a one-syllable word or in an accented syllable, the first vowel often represents its long sound and the second is silent. This holds true most often for the vowel digraphs ai, oa, ee, and ay combinations.

rain	boat	feet	day
meat	suit	sea	coal
soap	gray	train	

g. Each vowel letter may represent the soft schwa sound often heard in the unaccented syllable as in dis *ap* pear, tel *e* gram, and hap *pi* ness.

h. Y functions as a vowel when it concludes a word which has no other vowel (try), concludes words of more than one syllable (daddy), and when it follows another vowel (day).

i. When a vowel precedes the letter r, the vowel sound is neither long nor short, but has a new sound: *a* as in air, *a* as in car, *e* as in hear, *er* as in her, *ir* as in first, *ur* as in burn, and *or* as in horn. Study the word lists for more examples.

Sound Patterns

Common sound patterns along with sample words follow.

ad	*en*	*ell*	*am*	*old*
bad	Ben	bell	dam	cold
dad	den	cell	ham	bold
fad	hen	fell	jam	fold
lad	men	sell	lamb	hold
had	pen	tell	Pam	mold
mad	ten	well	Sam	sold
			ram	told

ake	*ent*	*ill*	*all*	*it*
bake	bent	Bill	ball	bit
cake	sent	fill	call	fit
fake	dent	kill	fall	hit
lake	rent	will	hall	kit
make	cent	pill	mall	Mit
rake	tent	till	tall	pit
take	went	sill	wall	sit

ay	at	an	et
bay	bat	can	bet
day	cat	ran	get
gay	fat	Dan	jet
hay	hat	fan	let
lay	mat	man	met
may	Nat	Nan	pet
pay	pat	pan	set
ray	rat	tan	wet
say	sat	van	yet
way			

Syllabication and Accent

The most common rules for *dividing words into syllables* are listed below:

1. When a word contains double consonants, the syllables are divided between these double letters, as in yellow, happy, runner, valley, ladder, bigger, puppy, rabbit, pretty, and butter.
2. When two different consonants come between two vowels, the syllables are usually divided between the consonants, as in donkey, signal, tonsil, perhaps, candy, pencil, farmer, surface, blanket, and lumber.
3. When a single consonant is between two vowels, the consonant usually begins the following syllable, as in begun, motor, stupid, final, cement, label, human, music, unit, and silent.
4. When a word contains prefixes such as ex or im or suffixes such as ly or ness, the prefix or suffix usually forms a separate syllable, as in exit, recite, unhappy, prepare, unkind, happiness, beautiful, useful, helpless, and foolish.
5. When a word ends in le, the consonant immediately preceding the le usually begins the last syllable, as in purple, handle, paddle, jungle, table, apple, simple, candle, and bottle.
6. Compound words are usually divided between their word parts or elsewhere if the word part has two syllables or more, as in basketball, horseshoe, mailman, playhouse, butterfly, rainbow, tiptoe, earphone, football, and pancake.
7. Consonant digraphs and consonant blends are considered as single consonants when words are divided into syllables, such as in the words machine, reply, hungry, enclose, anchor, and orchard.

The most common rules for *accenting words* follow:

1. The accent usually falls on or within the root word of a word containing a prefix or a suffix, such as in return or useful.
2. The accent usually falls on or within the first word of a compound word, such as horseback and football.

3. In a two-syllable word that functions as either a noun or a verb, the accent is usually on the first syllable when the word functions as a noun, such as in record (rec ord) and on the second syllable when the word functions as a verb (re cord).
4. In a two-syllable word containing a double consonant, the accent usually falls on the first syllable, such as in happy.
5. In a multi-syllable word ending in tion, the primary accent falls on the syllable preceding the tion, such as in vacation.
6. A final syllable containing a long vowel sound is usually accented, such as in parade and entertain.
7. When there is no other clue to a two-syllable word, the accent most often falls on the first syllable.

APPENDIX G

SAMPLE SENTENCES AND STORIES USING WORDS FROM FORGAN'S INITIAL 101 SIGHT WORD LIST

by Philip Kellerman

Listed below are 100 sentences and 10 stories which include only words from Forgan's Initial Sight Word List. These samples are provided to give you ideas for making your own sentences and stories using the words from the list. Of course, you can use these sentences and stories if you wish.

Sentences

1. I like you.
2. Look at that!
3. I give up!
4. There she was.
5. There it is!
6. I am ———————————.
         (child's name)
7. ——————————— is my sister.
        (sister's name)
8. ——————————— is my brother.
        (brother's name)
9. My friend is ———————————.
              (friend's name)
10. We run and play.
11. I play with ———————————.
             (pet's name)
12. Their home is new.
13. Soon she will run.

14 They went to play.
15. We can do that.
16. I go to work.
17. My ——————————— is very new.
        (child's favorite toy)
18. You did take some.
19. That was very good.
20. Bring some with you.
21. Come and get it.
22. They were good to me.
23. When will we go there?
24. He had work to do.
25. My home is your home.
26. Come to see me soon!
27. We like that new boy.
28. They will come and play.
29. His daddy can get them.
30. My daddy is at work.
31. We will look for you.
32. She will run by them.
33. They will eat with you.
34. I am a good boy.
35. I am a good girl.
36. Mommy and daddy like me.
37. My sister is a girl.
38. My brother is a boy.
39. I go out to play.
40. We have a new home.
41. We all like to eat.
42. She said I can bring him.
43. "Eat your ————————————" said his mommy.
                (child's favorite food)
44. I think she will get it.
45. They will get to use some.
46. Some of them came from her.
47. I can give some to him.
48. I would like to be me!
49. Do give one to your brother.
50. I think the boy said that.
51. Which one of you saw it?
52. Has he been to see you?
53. The girl will see me very soon.
54. I would like to see you there.
55. All of them will think about it.
56. I think I am a good boy.
57. They are going to bring ———————————— to eat.
                (name of favorite food)

58. I see a girl that I like.
59. She has not been a good girl.
60. I like to run with my —————————.
(child's pet)
61. We like to play with my ————————————.
(child's favorite toy)
62. We had to use some of them.
63. One boy went to look for her.
64. All we did was look at it.
65. This is a good one to have.
66. I would like to have a ————————————— one.
(child's favorite color)
67. I think I will look for that girl.
68. I am not about to work on it.
69. ————————————— has to bring this to my sister.
(friend's name)
70. When all of them come I will run.
71. A good boy will eat all he has.
72. I would like to jump up on you.
73. I would like to make this for my mommy.
74. We have a new one for you to use.
75. Then they had to go and look for him.
76. I would do it if I could do it!
77. If you see my brother make him come home.
78. You can make some if you would like to.
79. I like to run in and out and all about.
80. Take some and then eat them when you get home.
81. I think about them, but I can not see them.
82. As soon as we went, he came to our home.
83. ————————————— will give it to you if you are good.
(friend's name)
84. From his look I think he did not like me.
85. My daddy, mommy, brother, sister, ————————— and —————————
(friend's name)   (pet's name)
were with me.
86. I have to go but I will play with you soon.
87. He saw me and so he came to play with me.
88. They do not like to play when they are at home.
89. He did that when he came to see if we were home.
90. We would like to get one soon so we can eat it.
91. My daddy said we could jump on him and play with him.
92. I saw the boy get up as soon as he said that.
93. If you could run there then you could give it to them.
94. I would like to go to see her if my daddy is there.
95. She would like to jump up on it to see him eat it.
96. She would like to look at him but he would think she likes him.
97. As soon as I give some to you, you have to do some work.
98. I would like to go to see it when I come to be with you.

99. In our home my daddy will give my brother, sister, mommy, and me work to do.

100. I could eat at your home but if not I will eat with my mommy and daddy.

Stories

I Will Eat It

I like ————————. It is good. My mom will make it. My
        (favorite food)
sister will look at it. My brother will see it. My friend will think to take
it. My daddy will think to give it to ———————— and
                              (child's pet)
———————— will run with it from my home to play with it.
   (child's pet)
But I will get it and then eat it.

It!

I like to run. My brother likes to run. My sister likes to run. When
we run we look for it. We like to see it. We like to play with it. We jump
when we see it. It is our ————————.
        (child's pet)

I Like Her

I saw this new girl on my way home. I said to my sister that I like
her. My sister said that she is a good girl. I said that I would like to go
out and play with her. She said, "We will see her when we come home."
We went to see her as soon as we could. I like her.

I Like ————————
(child's favorite food)

I went to my friend's home to play. Her mommy, daddy, sister, and
brother were there. We went out to play. Soon her mommy said, "Come
to eat." We went in and saw what we were having to eat. It was
————————! We said, "good!" And it was very good. I
(child's favorite food)
would like to bring some home for you.

A New One!

I like my mommy and daddy. My daddy works. My mommy works at
home. But my mommy cannot work or play or jump. She can think about
her new one. Soon she will give my brother, sister, and me a new one!
A new one? What is this new one? We will soon see this new one. The
new one will be a new brother or sister!

176

I Am Me

I would like for you to play and do,
To jump out and all about.
To run for me or she or he,
For all to look — for all to see.
And if you could I think you would
Have said to all "I like to be me!"

My Home

When my daddy comes home from work he likes to see my mommy, brother, sister, and me. We like to see him. He is a good daddy. We like to play with him. We play when mommy makes some ————————
(child's favorite food)
to eat. Then mommy comes out to play. Then we all eat. We like our mommy and daddy.

Did You See Them?

———————————— said, "He is not there." I said, "So we will
(child's friend)
look for him." ———————————— said, "Did you see him?" "I do
(child's friend)
not see him," I said. "He will bring his sister," ———————— said.
(child's friend.
I said, "Do you see her?" "No, I do not see her."————————————
(child's friend)
said, "I have to go and work with my daddy." I said, "I will be here and see if they come. If they do we will come to your home and see you." "That is good," ———————— said.
(child's friend)

My Name Is ————————————
(child's name)

My name is ———————————. I am a ————————————. I like
(child's name)   (boy, girl)
to be good. I like to run and jump. I like to work then play. I like to think. I like to look at all I see! My mommy and daddy have not been at home. As soon as they come home, I will see them. I like them. I like to be good to them. They think I am a good ————————————. Will
(boy, girl)
you be as good as I am? You can — if you would like to.

To Be A Good Boy

I went to get my —————————— to use with ——————————.
            (child's favorite toy)   (child's friend)
He jumped up on it and then the ————————— would not work. I said to
                                    (toy)
him that he was not a good boy. I said to him that he could not use the
—————————. It was not for him to use. So I said to him to look for a
(toy)
new one, but he said he would not look for one for me. I said I did not
like him for that and that I would not play with him at all. I said to him
that as soon as he will get a new ————————— for me, then I would play
with him. He had to think about it. Then he said he would look for one
and bring one to me. He did look and soon he had one for me. I said
to him that was good to do. Our new ————————— was a good one and
                                        (toy)
we went to play with it.

APPENDIX H

SELECTED REFERENCE BOOKS FOR CHILDREN

This is a sample list of reference books. Refer to *Reference Books for Elementary and Junior High School Libraries* and/or *Guide to Reference Books* for more information. Both of these books are published by the American Library Association and should be available for reference in your local library.

Picture Dictionaries

Courtis, Stuart, and Garnett Watters. *Illustrated Golden Dictionary*. New York: Simon and Schuster, Inc.

MacBean, Dilla W. *Picture Book Dictionary*. Chicago· Children's Press Inc.

McIntire, Alta. *The Follett Beginning-to-Read Picture Dictionary*. Chicago: Follett Publishing Company.

Monroe, Marion, and W. C. Greet. *My Little Dictionary*. Glenview, Ill: Scott, Foresman and Company.

O'Donnell, Mabel and Wilhelmina Townes. *Words I Like to Read, Write, and Spell*. New York: Harper and Row, Publishers, Inc.

Parke, Margaret B. *Young Reader's Color-Picture Dictionary for Reading, Writing, and Spelling*. Illustrated by Cynthia and Alvin Koehler. New York: Grosset & Dunlap, Inc.

Scott, Alice, and Stella Center. *The Giant Picture Dictionary for Boys and Girls*. New York: Doubleday & Company, Inc.

Watters, Garnett, and Stuart Courtis. *The Picture Dictionary for Children*. New York: Grosset & Dunlap, Inc.

Wright, Wendell W. ed. *The Rainbow Dictionary*. Cleveland: The World Publishing Company.

Dictionaries for the Elementary School

Compton's Dictionary of the Natural Sciences. Chicago: F. E. Compton Co.
Compton's Illustrated Science Dictionary. Chicago: F. E. Compton Co.
Giant Golden Illustrated Dictionary, Stuart A. Courtis and Garnett Watters, (eds.).
   New York: Golden Press, Inc.
The Ginn Intermediate Dictionary. William Morris, Editor-in-Chief. Lexington, Mass.
   Ginn and Company.
The Holt Basic Dictionary of American English. New York: Holt, Rinehart and
   Winston, Inc.
The Holt Intermediate Dictionary of American English. New York: Holt, Rinehart
   and Winston, Inc.
Illustrated Golden Dictionary for Young Readers, rev. ed. Stuart A. Courtis and
   Garnett Watters, (eds.). New York: Golden Press, Inc.
Thorndike-Barnhart Beginning Dictionary, Edward L. Thorndike and Clarence L.
   Barnhart, (eds.). Chicago: Scott, Foresman and Company.
Thorndike-Barnhart Intermediate Dictionary, Edward L. Thorndike and Clarence
   L. Barnhart, (eds.). Chicago: Scott, Foresman and Company.
Webster's Dictionary for Boys and Girls. New York: American Book Company.
Webster's Elementary Dictionary. New York: American Book Company.
The Winston Dictionary for Schools. Thomas K. Brown and William D. Lewis,
   (eds.). New York: Holt, Rinehart and Winston, Inc.
The World Book Dictionary. Chicago: Field Enterprises, Inc.

Young Children's Encyclopedias

Childcraft — The How and Why Library. Chicago: Field Enterprises, Inc.
Compton's Children's Precyclopedia. Chicago: F. E. Compton Company.
The Golden Book Encyclopedia. New York: Simon and Schuster, Inc.

Encyclopedias for Elementary School Children

Book of Knowledge. New York: Grolier Society
Britannica Junior. Chicago: Encyclopedia Britannica Association.
Compton's Young Children's Precyclopedia. Chicago: F. E. Compton Company.
The Modern Century Illustrated Encyclopedia. Englewood Cliffs, N.J.: Scholastic
   Book Services.
Our Wonderful World. Chicago: Spencer Press, Inc.
The World Book Encyclopedia. Chicago: Field Enterprises, Inc.

Thesauri

In Other Words I. Beginning thesaurus for children in third and fourth grade. Chicago: Scott, Foresman and Co.
In Other Words II. Junior thesaurus for fifth and sixth grade. Chicago: Scott, Foresman and Co.

Atlases

Goode's World Atlas. Chicago: Rand McNally.
My First World Atlas. (Elem.) New York: McGraw-Hill.
Rand McNally World Atlas. Chicago: Rand McNally.
The World Book Atlas. Chicago: Field Enterprises, Inc.

APPENDIX I

SELECTED REFERENCES FOR PARENTS

Albrecht, Margaret. *Parents and Teen-agers: Getting Through to Each Other*. New York: Parents' Magazine Press.

Allen, Patricia. *Best Books for Children*. New York: R. R. Bowker.

Arbuthnot, May Hill. *Children's Reading in the Home*. Glenview, Illinois: Scott, Foresman and Company, 1969.

Baghban, Marcia. *How Can I Help My Child Learn to Read English as a Second Language?* Newark, Delaware: International Reading Association.

Beadle, Muriel. *A Child's Mind: How Children Learn During the Critical Years from Birth to Age Five*. New York: Doubleday, 1971.

Beck, Joan. *How to Raise a Brighter Child*. New York: Pocket Books, 1975.

Chan, Julie M. T. *Why Read Aloud to Children?* Newark, Delaware: International Reading Association, 1974.

Clarke, Louise. *Can't Read, Can't Write, Can't Talk Too Good Either*. Baltimore: Penguin Books, 1974.

DeFranco, Ellen B. and Evelyn M. Pickarts. *Dear Parents: Help Your Child to Read*. New York: American Book Company, 1972.

Dodson, Fitzhugh. *How to Father*. Los Angeles: Nash Publishing Company, 1974.

Dodson, Fitzhugh. *How to Parent*. Bergenfield, New Jersey: The New American Library, Inc.

Doman, Glenn. *How to Teach Your Baby to Read*. New York: Random House.

Frank, Fosette. *Your Child's Reading Today*. New York: Doubleday, 1969.

Getman, G. N. *How to Develop Your Child's Intelligence*. Luverne, Minnesota: Privately Printed, 1962.

Gilbert, Sara D. *Three Years to Grow: Guidance for Your Child's First Three Years*. New York: Parents' Magazine Press.

Glover, Leland E. *How to Give Your Child a Good Start in Life*. New York: Collier Books.

Glover, Leland E. *How to Guide Your School-Age Child*. New York: Collier Books.

Ginott, Haim. *Between Parent and Child*. New York: The Macmillan Company, 1965.

Gregg, Elizabeth and Members of the staff of the Boston Children's Medical Center. *What to Do when "There's Nothing to Do."* New York: Dell Publishing Company, 1968.

Hartley, Ruth E. and Goldenson, Robert M. *The Complete Book of Children's Play*. New York: Thomas Y. Crowell Co.

Hilsheimer, Geroge Von. *How to Live with Your Special Child*. Washington, D.C.: Acropolis Books Ltd.

Hoover, Mary B. *The Responsive Parent: Meeting the Realities of Parenthood Today*. New York: Parents' Magazine Press.

Hoover, Mary B. (ed.). *Guiding Your Child from 5 to 12: What Parents Need to Know During the Learning Years*. New York: Parents' Magazine Press.

Johnson, June. *838 Ways to Amuse a Child: Crafts, Hobbies, and Creative Ideas for the Child from 6-12*. New York: Collier Books.

Kronick, Doreen. *They Too Can Succeed; a Practical Guide for Parents of Learning-Disabled Children*. Belmont, California: Fearon Publishers.

Larrick, Nancy. *A Parent's Guide to Children's Reading*. New York: Doubleday and Company, Inc.

LeShan, Eda J. Natural Parenthood: *Raising Your Child without Script*. Bergenfield, New Jersey: The New American Library.

Matterson, E. M. *Play and Playthings for the Preschool Child*. Baltimore: Penguin Books.

180

Minton, Lynn. *Growing into Adolescence: A Sensible Guide for Parents of Children 11 to 14*. New York: Parents' Magazine Press.

Mogal, Doris P. *Character in the Making: The Many Ways Parents Can Help the School-Age Child*. New York: Parents' Magazine Press.

Murphy, John F. *Listening, Language and Learning Disabilities: A Guide for Parents and Teachers*. Cambridge, Mass: Educators Publishing Service, Inc.

National Education Association. *Get Involved in Your Child's School*. Washington, D.C.: National Education Association.

National Education Association. *Parents Involvement: A Key to Better Schools*. Washington, D.C.: National Education Association.

National Reading Center. *Helping the Beginning School Child with Reading*. Washington, D.C.: National Reading Center.

National Reading Center. *Parents Can Teach Pre-Reading Skills at Home*. Washington, D.C.: National Reading Center.

Neisser, Edith C. *Primer for Parents of Preschoolers*. New York: Parents' Magazine Press.

O'Conner, Grace. *Helping Your Children — A Basic Guide for Parents*. Austin, Texas: Steck-Vaughn, 1966.

Patterson, Gerald R. and Gullion, M. Elizabeth. *Living with Children*. Champaign, Illinois: Research Press, 1968.

Pickarts, Evelyn M. and Ellen B. DeFranco. *Parents, Children, and Reading*. New York: American Book Company, 1972.

Rogers, Norma. *What Books and Records Should I Get for My Preschooler?* Newark, Delaware: International Reading Association.

Sayler, Mary Lou. *Parents: Active Partners in Education*. Washington, D.C.: American Association of Elementary-Kindergarten-Nursery Educators, 1971.

Scargall, Jeanne. *1001 Ways to Have Fun with Children*. Toronto: Pagurian Press Limited, 1973.

Smith, Carl B. *Parents and Reading*. Newark, Delaware: International Reading Association, 1971.

Smith, Mildred Beatty. *Home and School Focus on Reading*. Glenview, Illinois: Scott, Foresman and Company.

Staiger, Ralph and John, David (ed.). *New Directions in Reading*. New York: Bantam Books.

Taylor, Katharine Whiteside. *Parents and Children Learn Together*. New York: Teachers College Press.

Valett, Robert E. *Prescriptions for Learning: A Parents' Guide for Remedial Home Training*. Belmont, California: Fearon Publishers.

Valett, Robert E. *Modifying Children's Behavior: A Guide for Parents and Professionals*. Belmont, California: Fearon Publishers.

APPENDIX J

A GRADED LIST OF THE NUMBERED IDEAS, ACTIVITIES, AND GAMES IN THIS BOOK

The following list can be used to determine what ideas, games, and activities you can use with your child. Refer to the sub-section of Chapter One, "The Arrangement of the Ideas, Games, and Activities in This Book," for a detailed description of the letter codes. Also refer to the portion of Chapter One, "How to Know What Ideas, Games, and Activities to Use with Your Child." Remember the ideas, games, and activities with the asterisks are the most important ones.

If your child is a preschooler, first grader, or in a higher grade but still reading at the readiness of first grade level, select appropriate activities from this list.

Chapter Two: Readiness

*1a	20a	39a	57a	75a
2a	21ab	40a	*58abc	76a
3ab	22ab	41a	59a	77a
*4a	23ab	42a	60a	78a
*5ab	24ab	43ab	61a	79a
*6a	25ab	44a	62a	*80ab
7a	26a	45a	63a	81abc
*8abc	27a	46a	64a	82a
*9abc	28a	47a	65ab	83ab
10a	29a	48a	66a	84a
*11abc	30a	49a	67ab	85ab
12a	*31abc	50a	68ab	86a
13ab	32ab	51a	69a	87a
14ab	33ab	52a	70a	88a
*15ab	*34ab	*53a	*71ab	89ab
*16ab	35a	*54abc	*72ab	90a
*17abc	36ab	55a	*73abc	91a
*18abc	*37a	56a	*74abc	92a
19ab	38ab			

Chapter Three: Phonics

93a	98ab	105ab	111a	117ab
94ab	99ab	106ab	112ab	118ab
95ab	100ab	*107abc	113a	119ab
96a	*101ab	108ab	114ab	120ab
97a	102ab	*109abc	115ab	*127ab
	104ab	110a	*116ab	130ab

Chapter Four:
Four Other Word Recognition Techniques

138a	144ab	150ab	158ab	169ab
*139a	145ab	151ab	*160ab	170ab
140a	146ab	152ab	162a	171ab
141a	147ab	153ab	164abc	173ab
142a	148ab	154ab	167a	175ab
143ab	149ab	155ab	168ab	176ab

Chapter Five: Comprehension

185a	189abc	204abc	216ab	224ab
186abc	190abc	*210abc	219ab	*225abc
187ab	*193abc	212abc	*220abc	*229abc
188ab	196ab	213ab	*221abc	230ab
	200abc	214abc	223abc	231abc

Chapter Six: Vocabulary

*239abc	*242abc	245ab	249a	257abc
*240abc	*243abc	*247abc	252abc	*258abc
*241abc	244ab	*248abc	*253abc	*261abc
			254abc	*263abc

Chapter Seven: Oral and Silent Reading

*265abc	*268ab	272ab	*277abc	283ab
*266ab	*270abc	273ab	280a	284ab
*267ab	271ab	274ab	*281ab	285ab
			*282ab	*287bc

Chapter Eight: Study Skills

*302abc	*310a		*317abc	324ab
*303abc	*314abc		318abc	325ab
				326ab

Chapter Nine: Interest in Reading

348abc	*350abc	*356abc	*358 abc	*367abc
349ab	*352abc	*357abc	*359abc	368abc
			366abc	369abc

If your child is reading at the second or third grade level, use these activities:

Chapter Two: Readiness

3ab	*16ab	25ab	*54abc	*73abc
*5ab	*17abc	*31abc	*58abc	*74abc
*8abc	*18abc	32ab	65ab	*80ab
*9abc	19ab	33ab	67ab	81abc
*11abc	21ab	*34ab	68ab	83ab
13ab	22ab	36ab	*71ab	85ab
14ab	23ab	38ab	*72ab	89ab
*15ab	24ab	43ab		

Chapter Three: Phonics

94ab	104ab	115ab	123b	131bc
95ab	105ab	*116ab	124b	*132bc
98ab	106ab	117ab	125b	133bc
99ab	*107abc	118ab	126b	134bc
100ab	108ab	119ab	*127ab	135b
*101ab	*109abc	120ab	128b	*136bc
102ab	112ab	121b	129b	*137bc
103b	114ab	122b	130ab	

Chapter Four: Four Other Word Recognition Techniques

143ab	151ab	159b	169ab	*177bc
144ab	152ab	*160ab	170ab	178bc
145ab	153ab	161ab	171ab	179bc
146ab	154ab	163bc	172bc	180bc
147ab	155ab	164abc	173ab	*181bc
148ab	156b	*165bc	174bc	182bc
149ab	157b	*166bc	175ab	*183bc
150ab	158ab	168ab	176ab	*184bc

Chapter Five: Comprehension

186abc	196ab	206bc	216ab	226bc
187ab	197bc	207b	217bc	227bc
188ab	198bc	208bc	219ab	228bc
189abc	199b	209b	*220abc	*229abc
190abc	200abc	*210abc	*221abc	230ab
*191bc	*201bc	211bc	222bc	231abc
192bc	202bc	212abc	223abc	232bc
193abc	*203bc	213ab	224ab	*233bc
194bc	204abc	214abc	*225abc	*238bc
195bc	205bc	215b		

Chapter Six: Vocabulary

*239abc	244ab	250bc	255bc	259bc
*240abc	245ab	251bc	256bc	260bc
*241abc	246bc	252abc	257abc	*261abc
*242abc	*247abc	*253abc	*258abc	*263abc
*243abc	*248abc	254abc		

Chapter Seven: Oral and Silent Reading

*265abc	271ab	276bc	*282ab	*287bc
*266ab	272ab	*277abc	283ab	288bc
*267ab	273ab	278bc	284ab	289bc
*268ab	274ab	279bc	285ab	*290bc
*270abc	275b	*281ab	*286bc	291bc
				293bc

Chapter Eight: Study Skills

*297bc	*303abc	. *315b	324ab	329bc
*298bc	311bc	*317abc	325ab	330bc
299bc	*312bc	318abc	326ab	331bc
*300bc	*313bc	319bc	*327bc	332bc
*302abc	*314abc	*321bc	*328bc	

Chapter Nine: Interest in Reading

341bc	346bc	*352abc	*357abc	365bc
342bc	347bc	353bc	*358abc	366abc
343bc	348abc	354bc	*359abc	*367abc
344bc	349ab	355bc	363bc	368abc
345bc	*350abc	*356abc	364bc	369abc

If your child is reading on the fourth, fifth, or sixth grade level, use these activities:

Chapter Two: Readiness

*8abc	*11abc	*18abc	*54abc	*73abc
*9abc	*17abc	*31abc	*58abc	*74abc
				81abc

Chapter Three: Phonics

*107abc	131bc	133bc	*136bc
*109abc	*132bc	134bc	*137bc

Chapter Four: Four Other Word Recognition Techniques

163bc	*166bc	*177bc	180bc	*183bc
164abc	172bc	178bc	*181bc	*184bc
*165bc	174bc	179bc	182bc	

Chapter Five: Comprehension

186abc	197bc	206bc	*220abc	*229abc
189abc	198bc	208bc	*221abc	231abc
190abc	200abc	*210abc	222bc	232bc
*191bc	*201bc	211bc	223abc	*233bc
192bc	202bc	212abc	*225abc	234c
*193abc	*203bc	214abc	226bc	235c
194bc	204abc	217bc	227bc	236c
195bc	205bc	218c	228bc	237c
				*238bc

Chapter Six: Vocabulary

*239abc	246bc	252abc	257abc	*261abc
*240abc	*247abc	*253abc	*258abc	*262c
*241abc	*248abc	254abc	259bc	*263abc
*242abc	250bc	255bc	260bc	264c
*243abc	251bc	256bc		

Chapter Seven: Oral and Silent Reading

*265abc	278bc	288bc	· 291bc	294c
*270abc	279bc	289bc	292c	295c
276bc	*286bc	*290bc	293bc	296c
*277abc	*287abc			

Chapter Eight: Study Skills

*297bc	305c	*314abc	322c	334c
*298bc	*306c	316c	323c	335c
299bc	307c	*317abc	*328bc	336c
*300bc	*308c	318abc	329bc	337c
301c	*309c	319bc	330bc	338c
*302abc	311bc	*320bc	331bc	339c
*303abc	*312bc	*321bc	333c	340c
304c	*313bc			

Chapter Nine: Interest in Reading

341bc	347bc	354bc	360c	365bc
342bc	348abc	355bc	361c	366abc
343bc	*350abc	*356abc	362c	*367abc
344bc	351c	*357abc	363bc	368abc
345bc	*352abc	358abc	364bc	369abc
346bc	353bc	*359abc		

Certificate of Award

for Reading Achievement

this certifies that

_____
name

is a member of the
10-Book Club

_____
Harry W. Forgan
Dr. H. W. Forgan
Reading Specialist

_____
Proud Parents

Certificate of Award

for Reading Achievement

this certifies that

_____
name

has learned all the
Basic Sight Words

_____
Henry W. Forgan
Dr. H. W. Forgan
Reading Specialist

_____
Proud Parents